To my husband, Ron,
my partner in this adventure

Contents

In Search
of an Answer

In 1995 we were finally free to go and solvent enough to afford it. We would visit the island where my father, Royse Rainey Gibson, had disappeared without a trace some 58 years before. We must have been quite a sight, my husband and I — sixty-something, in pretty good shape but not athletes, scrambling up a tundra-covered incline on Kanaga, an island near the middle of the Aleutian chain.

On his back, draped over his pack, Ron was carrying our raft. We had used it to row ashore from the float plane that brought us to this volcanic destination. Mark, the pilot, was unfamiliar with the harbor and wasn't sure if a change in the weather might dictate our pickup point. He had instructed us to be alert for the sound of an engine starting, a signal that weather was closing in. We were taking our water transport with us in case he had to move the plane to pick us up at a different point on the shoreline. I was carrying the oars and my own backpack.

The incline was steep but not high. The tundra-covered lava came down to the shoreline, and we soon discovered that the perpendicular climb would be an extra challenge. We looked for an opening so we could climb to the top. The tundra was awful to get through — about two feet deep, and thick. Adding to the depth was the summer growth of reeds, flowers and grasses.

We tried walking upright but it was hard to get a foothold, so we were pulling ourselves up hand over hand. We had to stop often to catch our breath.

Climbing the tundra on Kanaga Island, Summer 1995

When we were finally on top, we set off for the remains of the buildings that had housed a contingent of Navy personnel. Nearby would be the monument that recorded the disappearance of my father.

Almost all of the buildings were gone, razed by order of the Navy when war was declared against the Japanese. Standing amid the remaining pilings we looked up the hill and saw the monument. It was the strangest feeling to actually see it, although I had seen a photo and I knew what was engraved on it.

We struggled to the top of the hill, and when we got there I reached out to touch the bronze marker. It felt like the culmination of a lifetime of yearning for closure.

Family Beginnings

In 1900 my father was born to homesteaders Jim and Ellen Gibson in Kelly, Oklahoma, north of Bonham, Texas, where Jim's parents lived. Jim had a sister, Nellie, who was blinded when she was four years old. She had been sent to a special school someplace in Texas, where she not only learned to read braille but also became well-educated in history, geography and writing. When she returned to the family she brought those skills with her. She was much respected by her brother and was given the honor of naming each child born to Jim and Ellen. Royse Rainey, the firstborn of six, was named after a favorite teacher at the School for the Blind.

Labor was endless on homestead land, and Jim and Ellen were very grateful that Aunt Nellie was available to watch over this child, whose curiosity led him to an education. Her knowledge about the wider world piqued Royse's hunger to explore lands beyond the horizon. His formal schooling was spasmodic and amounted to about five years in a classroom.

Although he had never seen an ocean, he knew that the U. S. Navy would provide an opportunity for him to explore beyond the expansive prairie of Oklahoma. When Europe was building up to the First World War, he applied to join that branch of the service. He was only

16 years old, but by predating his birth date and with written parental permission he was old enough to volunteer. At the Recruit Depot in Oklahoma City, Royse presented his papers and received his train ticket and orders to report to the Navy Boot Camp in San Francisco.

In November of 1918 the war in Europe ended. Still in San Francisco, Royse finished Boot Camp and was learning procedures to be a hospital corpsman. When he had the opportunity, he explored the world around him. He rode on the ferry boat across San Francisco Bay and hiked to the top of Mt. Tamalpais, the local elevation that afforded a view of the steep hills of San Francisco to the south and the rolling terrain of the Napa Valley to the north.

Royse Rainey Gibson

He rode on the cable cars. He went to Chinatown, where he bought his sister a pair of silk slippers and a gold ring that cost $12.50.

With the end of the war, the United States had no more crucial need of military manpower. Royse was discharged. And in July of 1919 he came home.

Jim and Ellen's son had grown taller. Eventually he would reach his full height at 6 feet 2 inches. And he brought stories to tell his family about the places he had seen. He showed them souvenir postcards of ships and sights. His family pored over the pictures and marveled at the information.

* * *

Royse had tasted adventure and he wanted more of it. Because he had a good service record and showed promise, his application for re-enlistment in the Navy, which now needed only his signature, was accepted. He waited for the notice that would take him back to wider adventures.

In the lull between ripening and harvesting crops was an opportunity to bring extra money into the household. Jim and Ellen contracted to go south to Texas where there was a bumper crop of cotton waiting to be picked.

It's wearisome work. When the pods open and the fluff spills out, it seems simple to pull it off and stuff it into a bag. But the pod openings are sharp, and without gloves fingers would be bleeding in no time. The sack that trails along behind is heavy and cumbersome. The scales are at the ends of the rows and someone is there to weigh and record the weight of the sack. Ellen could fill her sack with a record 90 pounds in a day. The rest of the family did well to pick a third of that amount.

In 1920 there was a respite on Christmas Day. Royse decided he and his brothers should mark the holiday by doing something memorable. It was cold, and ice was floating in some of the sheltered spots in the Red River. He led his brothers to the bank and stripped off his clothes. Then he announced that they'd go swimming. Following his example they all jumped naked into the river. The excursion was over in a split second.

While the family was camped near the cotton field, notification came for Royse to report to Oklahoma City for re-enlistment into the Navy. A train ticket was included in the envelope. Two days after the Red River swim his parents delivered him to the railroad station in Bonham, Texas. They knew that this time their departing son would return only as a visitor.

* * *

Ione Mary Steetle and Royse Rainey Gibson met on a blind date in San Diego. I don't know who introduced them or how long they knew each other before they went to Yuma in June of 1929 to get married. By then Royse was a Pharmacist's Mate First Class in the U. S. Navy, and advancing in his medical specialty. He was stationed at Mare Island, a little northeast of San

Ione and Royse

Francisco, when daughter Ellen was born at the Vallejo Naval Hospital in August, 1930. In 1931 they were sent to Honolulu, where I was born a year later.

I was just a few months old when he was transferred to Annapolis, Maryland. This was early in FDR's administration, and to alleviate the hopelessness of the Depression, Franklin and Eleanor invited the public to file through the downstairs reception room of the White House, where they would shake hands and provide assurance that the new President cared about their welfare. It was quite natural for FDR to say, "Let me hold the baby." This episode became part of our family lore.

Three years later when Royse was transferred to Honolulu again, our little family drove across the country. I don't know what make the car was, but I can remember sitting on Daddy's lap and helping him steer. There was a circular design on the dashboard on the passenger side. When I sat on Mama's lap I pretended that too was a steering wheel.

We stopped in Oklahoma to see Royse's family, who were farming and raising cattle. The gathering of the clan extended to several grandchildren. Ellen couldn't be contained and our parents kept her in a harness. My grandmother had a fit.

"They lead her around just like a dog," she said.

Mama said, "Well, you're welcome to chase her."

My baby-talk name for Ellen was "Ollen." It got shortened to "On." She went to first grade in Honolulu and I went to a preschool for a few hours a week. We lived in a two-bedroom house with little furniture. I remember that Daddy played a game with us — he would say the name of a state and we'd tell him the capital. I can remember riding his foot as he sat on one of the kitchen chairs. When he said "Arkansas," I said "Little Rocker" and pictured the small rocking chair (and doll crib) he had made for On and me.

On was "hell on wheels" and really kept Mama hopping. I don't remember this, but Mom said that she'd take off one of her "go aheads" (rattan shoes) and use it for a paddle.

One day we were getting ready to go to the beach, and although it would be years before On had anything to cover up, she threw a fit and wouldn't budge until she had a top to go with her swim trunks. I can picture my Daddy standing in the doorway while Mama sat at the sewing machine in the kitchen putting together unnecessary halter tops for both of us.

In 1935 or '36 the four-engine China Clipper, one of the largest planes of its time, landed at Pearl Harbor and invited visitors to go on board. I held my Daddy's hand as we walked up the narrow aisle.

In 1937 he was transferred to San Diego and I started kindergarten there. We lived with my grandmother on Island Avenue.

Among the things Daddy unpacked from Hawaii was a skull he had recovered from below the Pali cliff near Honolulu. (In 1795 as part of his effort to unify Hawaii, King Kamehameha had driven the enemy troops over this cliff, where they fell to the valley floor below. In 1898 a road construction project unearthed more than 800 skulls there.) On liked to be terrorized by the skull, and Daddy held it in his hand and chased her around the house. I can remember her laughing and yelling "Stop!" And when our Daddy did stop, she went right back to baiting him.

A Sunday paper came to Grandma's house. On those mornings On and I would get in bed with Mama and Daddy and he'd read the funnies to us. I suspect he inserted his own comments that weren't entirely appropriate for young ears. Mom told me later that he'd also recite lines from poems to

Estelle and Ellen

7

his own purposes: "Away to the window he flew like a flash, tore open the shutters and threw up the hash."

* * *

The last memory I have of Daddy was in the bedroom of my Grandma's house. I came into the room and he and Mama were sitting on a trunk beside the closet door. She was leaning against him and crying. He had his arm around her. I said, "What's the matter?" And she said, "Daddy's going away."

I pondered that as I looked at them. I didn't know men could cry.

Prelude to War

Domestically, Roosevelt's "New Deal" was the focus of his administration when he was elected in 1932. But he and his advisors were well aware of the threat that Japan's expanding empire posed for the United States when that aggressing nation invaded Manchuria in 1931.

Reeling from the Depression, our leadership didn't publicly address the turmoil that was enveloping Asia. But the administration had put plans in place for U. S. protection if our country came under threat. The Aleutian Islands that could be a conduit from Japan to Alaska could be used in reverse if the ultimate need arose to invade Japan. For this to happen, the weather and terrain had to be studied.

In the 1930s relatively few Americans would have known where the Aleutian Islands were.

9

The chain of islands stretched a thousand miles through the ice-packed waters from the Alaska Peninsula across the Bering Sea. There were Japanese boats in the fishing territory, whose movements and communication needed to be monitored. And with an eye to building airfields, the weather cycle would be recorded and the terrain would be studied.

It wouldn't take many personnel to gather this information. So in October of 1937 a crew of eight men was sent to Kanaga, a small island in the middle of the Aleutian chain, just west of Adak. The term of their duty was to be one year, during which they would record the movement of fishing boats, monitor radio messages and keep track of weather patterns.

Two of the eight men would not be assigned to those duties. One was Clyde Musick, the cook. And one was Royse Gibson, the medic.

The mission was termed "secret." Until the Panay Incident in December of 1937, when an American gunboat was "accidentally" sunk by a Japanese warship in the Yangtze River near Nanking, China, there would be no overt reason for the United States to prepare to defend itself from outside aggression.

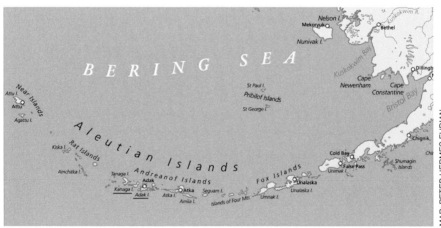

Kanaga Island, near Adak, would be investigated as a possible site for an airbase.

Letters Home

From October 4 to November 5, 1937, as he traveled by U. S. Navy ship up the Pacific Coast of the United States, at first not knowing where he was headed, Royse Rainey Gibson wrote letters to his wife, Ione, and their daughters, Ellen and Estelle. The handwritten letters were mailed, and his wife's letters were delivered to him, when the ship put into port. Ione kept his communiques. The 19 letters reproduced here provide insight at a very personal level into a little-known U. S. Navy mission during the lead-up to World War II.

The USS Portland, on which Royse Gibson traveled up the Pacific coast to the Puget Sound Naval Shipyard in Bremerton, Washington

11

Aboard USS Portland in Long Beach   Monday, 4 Oct 1937

My Dearest Ione & Babies:

Right after I left you I saw CPhM* Day, who is on the Penna. He told me this job might not last over six weeks. That it would pay $1.95 a day subsistence and that there is nothing to spend money for. Sounds like I should come back with a pot full of money.

I got a Northampton boat soon after you left. When I got on board I was given a new set of orders and sent over to this ship. I like it fine so far. Dr. Robertson from Annapolis is on here. Van Gage left for the Arizona some time ago. Harrell has been paid off for some time. Dr. Robertson wants me to stay on here for duty. I think I would like it.

We take on stores tomorrow and get under way Thursday – just like I told you. No one seems to know what this duty is all about. Three of us were in to see the Capt this morning. He doesn't know how many are in the draft nor what the duty is like. Must be a secret.

What time did you get home? Have any trouble? I suppose Fleming is well on his way to Mare Island now. Have you gotten over your moody spell yet? Mine is just beginning. The people on here tell me that Alaska has two kinds of weather. Foggy & stormy. Long underwear is hard to get now. You will have time to get an answer to me if we don't leave before Thursday.

Kisses & Love to you all,
Royse

*CPhM is *Chief Pharmacist's Mate,* a rate of Naval Hospital Corpsman.

Aboard the USS Portland in Long Beach   Wednesday, 6 Oct 1937

My dearest Ione & Babies:

I have just come ashore. The first time I have been to the top side since I left you. Will certainly be a lazy bones before this trip is over. I stay around the sick bay in the morning, and sleep all afternoon.

We leave tomorrow morning. If you write, send the letter to the USS Portland, Navy Yard Bremerton, Wash. Have not been able to find out a thing about the nature of the duty on this trip.

The Portland is a good ship. Has nice quarters and feels good. As I told you, have not seen the top side since I got on board. I don't know anything about the ship. She was launched in 1932.

Have been reading a lot the last three days. Mostly good magazines and one book.

We won't stop at S. F. The trip up will take about four days. Will be my first time in Bremerton.

One of the CPOs* who was in Alaska two or three years ago tells me that it is not so cold, but is continually foggy and lots of wind. We will have to wait and see. Will have a letter off to you when the ship docks.

Love & a kiss for each of you,
Royse

---

*CPOs are *Chief Petty Officers*.

U. S. S. PORTLAND GOES NORTH UNDER SECRET ORDERS

LOS ANGELES, Oct. 8 (A.P.)— The Times says a spokesman for the U. S. fleet disclosed tonight the heavy cruiser Portland left San Pedro under secret orders yesterday on a confidential mission in the Alaskan-Aleutian islands area. He declared the cruise is not connected with the Sino-Japanese war situation.

The Portland, one of the navy's newest 10,000-ton treaty cruisers, carries four scouting seaplanes and is armed with nine eight-inch guns. Her speed is 33 knots.

The spokesman said she would put into Puget Sound Navy Yard, probably tomorrow, to drydock for bottom cleaning, painting and minor overhaul and to take on special personnel and equipment.

The navy recently announced plans to station permanently two squadrons of huge long-range flying boats at Sitka and it was suggested that their operation would necessitate accurate meteorological information from the Aleutian-Bering Sea "weather factory," possibly requiring the stationing of observers on the lonely islands.

Ione saved a newspaper clipping about Royse's mission; October 8, 1937.

Aboard the USS Portland, at sea   Saturday, 9 Oct 1937

My dearest Ione & Babies:

We are off the coast of Oregon this evening. Will be in Bremerton about 3 pm tomorrow. The weather has been fine, not a rough wave on the whole trip. No fog. We stayed close to the shore all the way until sometime last night.

Have not been able to get a bit of information about what I am going to do yet. About all that I have done so far has been to sleep, eat, and read awhile. I have an idea that next week I will really go to work.

Harry Van Gage was on this ship for a while. So were Harrell & Dreyer. All of this crew speaks well of Harrell. The Chiefs (about 30 of them) are a reserved bunch, only two of them have spoken to me so far. I'm really afraid that I smell bad.

You made pretty good time on the way back. I woke up two or three times during the night and would wonder just where you would be.

As near as I can figure it this ship is going up to Dutch Harbor with supplies and I will probably be on it, too. And then across to the Aleutian Islands and on back — and I won't be on it. The ship will be back in San Pedro about the middle of November.

There is no CPhM on board here. Sort of wish I could stay on board. I like Dr. Robertson — he is sort of bad at times, but I think he is OK.

The library on here is not so much. Of course the good books never reach the library until they have been read and re-read by the officers.

We had inspection this morning. I did not go — too much trouble. This afternoon Menifee (1stCl) and me inspected the medical storeroom. I have been going over their lab material. Am making a big headway with this. Will write some more tomorrow before mailing this.

                 Pleasant dreams!
                 Royse

15

USS Portland, Navy Yard Bremerton   Sunday, 10 Oct 1937

Dearest Babies:

We are in Bremerton Navy Yard now. Got in here about 4:00 pm. This is a pretty country. Tall pine trees on all sides. The Navy Yard reminds me a lot of Mare Island. Have not been off the ship. I went to the top side this morning for a few minutes. Lost the anchor off my cap, so that means I must spend 65 cents for a new one tomorrow.

Mail has not come on board yet. It will be just my luck not to get a letter tonight. I am new on here so they will hold my letters up until last. No mail going out at this hour, so I can hold this letter up until late tonight.

This afternoon I wrote out the questions for a man taking the exam for Second Class PhM. Will know tomorrow where I am going. No more news so far, so I will mail this now.

Mucho Amor,

Royse R

1930s postcard showing Bremerton and the Navy Yard

USS Portland, Navy Yard Bremerton   Tuesday, 12 Oct 1937

My dearest Ione and Girls:

No letter from you yesterday when we got in here. It came today however. I wrote to you yesterday and mailed it. Had to put the finishing lines in it in a hurry so you can see by the way I signed it.

Well, the trip up here was fine. We didn't even have a white cap the whole trip.

Yesterday was spent in getting organized and today in running around after supplies, and so far I have not accomplished a thing. Saw Dr. Jordan, who was at Md a few years ago. He is the same old piss ant as ever. There's another medic here with my name – CPhM Gibson. I met his wife. She's a real nice woman.

This morning I went to the District Medical Officer's office and got an order for medicines. Have not gotten them yet.

There are eight of us in this party. 1 Lieutenant, 3 Chiefs, 1 cook, and the others are blue jackets. I don't like this Lt. Kellerman. May change my opinion after a while. We are to get $1.85 per day sustenance and possibly $2.10. We figure we can eat for $28 or $30 per month. If we can, we will save a little money.

I paid my mess bill this morning for the time I've been on here. It was $6.00 (50 cents per day), which is too much. I believe I can get part of it back. At any rate I am almost broke.

We leave here Thursday for Kanaga Island, Alaska, on the 180th meridian and between the 50th and 55th parallel. We will establish a base for gathering weather data.

Now about money. I'll leave here broke. If the mess wants any more money from me they will either take it from my pay or I'll have to send a letter to you and ask you to pay it for me. Sad situation, isn't it.

Don't know whether I'll have enough blankets. Hope so. I don't think that I'll freeze at any rate.

Our pay will have to be sent to a bank here in Bremerton. Mail will go and come about twice a month – weather permitting.

The chief radioman (Cunningham) tells me there is a fox ranch manager on the island of Kanaga. I don't know anything about him except he does have a radio. The name is Clark and it's possible I can send messages to you through him.

The only thing is I want to sleep in your arms and warm your feet. I have not slept warm since I've been here.

So you got all the trash out? Did you have any growls? That re-minds me – garbage goes out tomorrow. There is no more to tell you tonight – will read awhile and then go to bed.

Love & pleasant dreams,
Royse

USS Portland, Navy Yard Bremerton   Wednesday, 13 Oct 1937

My dearest Ione and girls:

Today has been another tough one for me. Over to Seattle again and spent the day running around. Got arctic shoes for all the gang. We are supposed to get heavy shirts and windbreakers next. Have not received a piece of heavy underwear yet. May have to draw a couple of suits on the way up.

We won't leave here tomorrow – possibly not until after the 19th. Well, as long as I am away I may as well be in Alaska. Have you looked it up on the map yet? It is Kanaga Island on the 180th meridian and about 52nd parallel. We will be about 500 miles from Dutch Harbor.

All my medical stores are packed. I'll have to get them on board tomorrow, then we have to get a physical exam and have our teeth examined. There is one syphilitic in the party – he may not go along.

The officer in charge told me that there will be no firearms allowed in the party. That suits me fine, because I won't have a desire for a rifle – and have no business with one. Will have to get along with a slingshot or bow-and-arrow.

News is sort of at a standstill. Mornings here are foggy and are cold enough to make the teeth chatter. This bay here is calm. There are pine trees on all sides and plenty of them, too. I do so wish you could see this part of the country. Perhaps you can come up here in March and we can see some of it on the way down. I should get transportation from here to San Francisco when my time is up.

More about Washington. Remember how colorful the trees around Annapolis were after frost? Well, there are a few bright trees here and numerous pines (fir) and just as tall as the books say they are, too. You could certainly get a Christmas tree here and a good one, too.

The allotment to the bank in Annapolis runs out in January. I am turning all my pay over to a bank here in Bremerton. They in turn will send it on to you or leave it ride as you see fit. I'll give you all the information in another letter. After the account in Md has been cleared up I would close it out and start doing all banking in San Diego.

I see lots of Eskimo moccasins. I'd like to get some for you, but I'd rather wait and deal with the Eskimos. Give me your shoe sizes (you and the girls in inches — actual length of feet).

I don't know when the checks from the paymaster will start coming to you. Should be in by the 5th of November.

As usual you were right. Wish I had the corduroy outfit, and if we don't leave until Monday, you would have had time to get them up here. Too late now. Will write every day until the last mail.

Love and kisses to each of you —
Poppy

USS Portland, Navy Yard Bremerton   Thursday, 14 Oct 1937

My dearest Ione:

    This will be the last letter for a while. We leave tomorrow noon.

    The allotment to you fell through as I have two out already, so it looks bad for you. However, I am transferring my pay (all of it) to the National Bank of Commerce, Bremerton, Washington, and they in turn are to send you $100.00 per month and are to pay my portion of the rations. You have the privilege of checking against the account. Will send you all the information tomorrow – you won't get it until after the Portland gets back to Seattle some time in November.

    I have to go ashore for some stuff for the Lieut-in-charge, so will be on my way. Will mail this on the way over. They tell me the trip across is going to be pretty rough.

    Am sorry I do not have time to write any more.

    You do as you like with the pictures. Am keeping the one you don't like. Ellen, you are doing real swell with your writing. Are you still going to Sunday School? Estelle, you must write, too, and you two girls remember I am going to be up pretty close to Santa Claus. Perhaps I can say a few words to you over the radio on Xmas Day. I hope so.

    Happy birthday, Mama mine.

              Love & kisses for all of you.
              Tomorrow I will feel pretty low.
              Royse

USS Portland, Navy Yard Bremerton   Thursday, 14 Oct 1937

Mama Dearest:

The letters with yours and Ellen's came in today and I am always happy to hear from you. The proofs are all good. You look delicious in all of them. I'll let you make the decision because you can have a little criticism, where I will not take anyone into confidence on here.

Had to go out into town (Bremerton) this morning. It is certainly a one-horse town. Very much like Annapolis. The town is right against the gate. Two streets and that is all of it — just three or four blocks. I like this country, because there is lots of timber. There is lots of fog and chilly mornings.

We leave here tomorrow at noon, go to Dutch Harbor, Alaska, and then on to Kanaga Island. The ship will stay with us until we are established, then they leave us to the cold wind. This will probably be the last letter until about the first of November. A fur boat will make Kanaga some time before the first of the year and then we are frozen in for a while.

You should see the heavy stuff we have: oilskins, fur-lined coats, heavy boots, socks, and all that stuff. I really don't know how much stuff we really have.

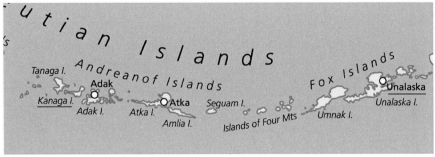

Dutch Harbor, on Unalaska Island, would be the last stop before arrival at Kanaga Island.

If I can, I'm going to re-enlist three months ahead of time. That will boost my retirement time for three months. What do you think of it?

This card is for your signature. Send it with the signed letter to the bank in Bremerton. Wish you would leave me a few dollars balance, because I may want it when I come back through here. As for souvenirs and furs, I'll get what I can for you three. Hope I can contact you often through the Clarks. Am almost certain that I can.

Have not had a good night's sleep since the Thursday before I left you. Some nights I can't go to sleep, others I sleep cold. Have dreamed of you nearly every night since I left.

This bunch of CPOs are very aloof. Well, I don't smell any worse than they do.

Nothing more to tell you, Mummer mine. So off to bed.

Pleasant dreams.
Royse

Does Freddy still have his car? How are the peas, beans, and tomatoes? Also the sweet potatoes? The potato vine in the back should be ready to dig up now.

Royse

USS Portland, at sea   Wednesday, 20 Oct 1937

My dearest Ione & Babies:

Your last letter came about the time we sailed from Bremerton. We left the Navy Yard about 4 PM. Made good time until yesterday. Yesternoon the sea got rough so we had to live on sandwiches and bread. Have not set the table all day today, and there is no relief in sight. So far I have not been seasick at all. We are in the storm center of the North Pacific. We lost twenty barrels of fuel oil which we had on board, and one of the compartment doors was smashed in by the waves. Not much damage done after all.

I want to mail this in Dutch Harbor, so you will have the postmark on it. I suppose the proofs of the girls are in Bremerton. I won't get them until about the first of December – if then. So you do as you see fit. I told you the allotment to the Annapolis bank runs out in January, so keep all the insurance paid up from Vallejo and the Bank in Bremerton.

Have heard all kinds of tales about the island we are going to. The name is Kanaga. It is about 500 miles from Dutch Harbor in the Aleutian chain. We have plenty of good food and coal on board for the whole stay.

May as well tell you now that the time up here will be at least a year. Didn't know it until a day before we left. My pay now is $156.50 plus $2.10 per day for chow, which is $63 per month, which puts us in the big money class of $219.50 a month. My expenses here are going to be nothing, so I am leaving it to you to do the money worrying. I drew $48 just before I left, so I am well fixed.

You should see the clothing we have. Heavy boots, socks, wind-proof clothing, sheepskin coats, and long underwear and woolen shirts. We will probably get to Dutch Harbor about Friday or Saturday, 23rd of Oct.

Nothing more to write tonight. Will write more when we anchor. We stop in Dutch Harbor first, and then go to Kanaga a day or two later.

Pleasant dreams.

Royse

USS Portland, Dutch Harbor, Alaska   Friday, 22 Oct 1937

My dearest Ione and Girls:

We got in here this morning about 9:30. Have not been to the top side yet to see what the place is like. Can see numerous little islands all around and all of them are snow-capped. There are no trees or even shrubbery, plenty of moss and grass, so we don't want to live up here.

The trip up was a whiz. We left Bremerton on the 15th (Friday). The sailing was fine until Tuesday noon, when the wind came up and it was sure enough rough. Somehow I never lost a meal. Was a little nauseated several times and had to take salts every day. We spent two days just making headway.

We have 200 barrels of fuel oil and gasoline on the fantail. The oil got loose and churned around. We lost 20 barrels of oil. That is one reason for not making any headway. We had to travel slow to keep the oil on board.

The Navy has a radio station over here. No PhM here, however. I believe you would like this town of Dutch Harbor. Just a handful of houses and a long warehouse on the dock. The Tanager is in here – it is a mine sweeper from Honolulu. Bricker is on board. He is over here this afternoon. Seems good to see him.

Postcard from the late 1930s showing Dutch Harbor on Unalaska Island

We leave tomorrow for Kanaga Island. We (Portland) stop at a little place about 40 miles from Kanaga and transfer all of our stuff to the Tanager and then we go to Kanaga on the Tanager. After that it is all isolation for us until next March or April. Mail may come in for us sometime in November or December. Hope to get a letter from you then.

Am sending you a Portland envelope and one to your friend Dorothy Hastings, so you may deliver mail to her and get jealous, but try to keep your friend Martha from going berserk.

As usual there is nothing in the line of news to tell after a few days at sea, and I have to make some ointments, so I'll close for the time and try to get this in the Dutch Harbor Post Office.

It is raining now and is cold to me. Menifee just came back from the beach. He tells some glowing tales about how primitive the place is. This town here, Unalaska, is the place where Dangerous Dan McGrew was killed off, so I am told. Came ashore at 6:00 this evening. This town of Unalaska is a whiz. I suppose Alaska is the last frontier. It is too dark to see anything, so I'll have to wait until tomorrow to ask a lot of foolish questions from someone who has seen it all.

Pleasant dreams and all of my love
to all of you.
Royse

Kanaga Island, Territory of Alaska   Sunday, 24 Oct 1937

My dearest Babe & Babies:

We left Dutch Harbor yesterday at 1:00 PM and anchored here 24 hours later. This place is not so bad so far. We have a very warm house, plenty of blankets, good mattresses and twenty tons of coal.

We left the ship right after chow at noon and brought stores over all afternoon — just like unpacking our stuff after we got back from Honolulu.

Here's the final group that will be together on Kanaga: Lt. Kellerman, C.Radioman Cunningham, C.Aerographer Cowell, myself, Cook I/Class Musick, Radioman I/Class Erwin, Aerographer 3C Rodman, and Southerland, Seaman I/C. Already there is a petty scrap brewing. I'm sitting on the sideline watching.

This island is owned by the U. S. Government and leased by a Mr. Bowman, who raises blue foxes. The island is about 15 miles wide and 30 miles long. The station has four or five buildings, a chicken house and pens. The foxes live under the house we are living in. I saw a very pretty one this afternoon.

It is bedtime, so I'll write more tomorrow.

Royse

1940s postcard showing an Aleutian arctic blue fox

Kanaga Island, Territory of Alaska   Monday, 25 Oct 1937

Dearest Babe & Babies:

Last night I was tired and could not go to sleep. Tonight I am tired and sleepy, but do not dare to go to bed because the others are working and it would not be right for me to turn in now.

Today I cleaned the shack where we are to live. Am really tired from sweeping and lifting crates. Today has been cold and windy. Squalls of wind, rain, and sleet. After this week we will be fixed pretty well. Just like when we move from one house to another.

I really should tell you more about this island in this letter. Have not had time to get out yet. The Portland leaves tomorrow or Wednesday and the Tanager leaves Thursday or Friday, then we are all alone for the Winter. Hope to tell you all about this place before the last mail leaves.

Saw an eagle, two hawks, lots of geese, and three or four foxes today. There is supposed to be good fishing and duck shooting on this island. There are a few hair seals here, too. We are allowed to kill hair seal. I want a hide for a rug. Eagle feet are worth 50 cents a pair. There is a bounty on them. Eagles eat fish, baby seals, foxes, and water birds.

PHOTO: DFIKAR

A "hair seal" can be any of several species, including a harbor seal like the one shown here.

Next week I move my bunk into the same quarters with Mr. Kellerman. He wants me to set the sick bay up near him. That means I'll have to keep his bunk cleaned up and his room swept out.

Well, Mommy, we have been separated less than a month and I am beginning to pretend to be asleep on your arm. Still, I'd rather be here than on a destroyer in Panama. Tomorrow I am to go to the Tanager to check stores. Will freeze my legs off, I am certain. Pleasant dreams to you all and a kiss for each of you.

I love you,
Royse

P. S. Will you send a Hospital Corps handbook (there are two of them in the books) and a laboratory book by either Stitt or Todd & Stanford. And the Arithmetic – there are two of them – one by Hamilton and the other by Wentworth & Smith. I'd rather have the Wentworth & Smith. And two packages of envelopes to fit paper of this size. That is three books and two pkgs of envelopes in all. And any snapshots you have of you and the babies. The address:

Royse R. Gibson, CPhM
c/o Commandant, 13th Nav Dist
Seattle, Washington

And are you getting the money alright? There is a tug boat coming up from Dutch Harbor sometime next month.

Love & Mootzies,
Poppy

Have not shaved for three days now. Wonder if I can hold out until Christmas.

Kanaga Island, Territory of Alaska   Saturday, 30 Oct 1937

My dearest Ione:

Today is your Birthday, isn't it? Have a nice Birthday party? I doubt if you have made much of a day of it. Started to send you a radio greeting. Cost too much. You could have silk stockings for quite a while on the money it would take.

Well, the Tanager is still here. It will leave us on Thursday and then we will be holed up until sometime in March. I don't think the Swallow will be up here until after March. There will be boats to Dutch Harbor all of the year.

My detail here is: Help the cook and clean the house — just like home, isn't it? Today I swept the place and peeled the squash. About all I do is to clean and drink coffee. Yesterday we carried tons of stores and restowed them in our storehouse. I went to the top of a mountain and took a look at an active volcano. It smokes sometimes.

This letter isn't much. I have just finished washing my self and clothes and it is after 11:00 PM, so perhaps I'd better go to sleep and do some more writing tomorrow. I have not shaved for a week today. If I can keep it up, won't I have a real beard?

Royse

Kanaga Island, Territory of Alaska   Sunday, 31 Oct 1937

Dear Babe,

We got here just a week ago today, and four weeks ago today I left you. Does it seem so long to you?

This morning we got up early and worked just the same. I went out to the Tanager to see Bricker. Some of the men on the Tanager shot an eagle yesterday. He measured 6 ft. 1 in. from wing tip to wing tip. Pretty good size bird. Coming back my cap blew off and went into the water. It drifted ashore, so I immediately washed it up and hung it behind the stove to dry.

This afternoon three of the men went out hunting. Of course all they saw was a few seagulls and an eagle or two. They fired about 75 shots and hit nothing. The cook and myself are going out some afternoon just to see what we can see. The story is: an Eskimo graveyard on one side of the island, an eagle's nest near our camp, an active volcano about fourteen miles away. Streams with lots of trout. Some placer gold and ducks and geese to be shot at. I sort of wish I had a rifle – but after all, what good would it do me to kill a poor goose?

Tonight is Halloween, isn't it? Any banshees around tonight? No more news tonight.

Royse

Kanaga Island, Territory of Alaska   Monday, 1 Nov 1937

Dearest Mommy,

Another day has passed. Nothing of interest today. Have lots of
wind. I went over a hill near the house today. There is a tall coarse
grass all over the land. Under the grass is a moss (tundra moss). The
ground is spongy and it makes walking very tiresome. The wind blows
about 40 miles per hr. Today we had fog, snow, sleet, rain & hail as
well as sunshine and wind. About 6:00 there wasn't even a breeze.

I found a joint of a whale backbone today. Have it as a door stop.
Tonight I washed clothes and cleaned up. I brought four sacks of coal
up and got pretty dusty. The Tanager is due to leave here Thursday, I
think.

A few lines about this island and us. Kanaga Island is about perhaps
30 miles long, by 15 miles wide, is of volcanic origin, has an active
volcano on the north end of it. All the vegetation is coarse grass and
tundra moss. There are no trees or shrubs.

The Alaska Trading Company has stocked it with blue foxes. There
are no other animals on it except for a herd of goats, which are here

PHOTO: U. S. NAVY

Aerial photo of Kanaga Island. Mount Kanaga volcano is on the right.

for milk. The bird life consists of a good number of eagles and ravens, as well as seagulls and other sea birds, such as geese & ducks. People tell me there a are a few ptarmigan. I have never seen one.

The main part (of our camp) consists of a dock, three or four storehouses, a few fox breeding pens, two trappers' cabins (we are in one of them). There is a chicken pen and house here, too. No chickens. The company has tried raising rabbits for fox food, but the rabbit didn't have a chance. Too cold and windy for chickens. They have to ship in grain and hay for the goats.

The caretaker, his wife, and an old fellow are stationed here, and our party of eight. Also six trappers are about all the people within miles of us. Seventeen people on an island of 450 square miles – about 26 square miles apiece.

The trapping begins about the middle of December and ends 1st of Feb – about 45 days. They expect to take about 1000 pelts (a pelt is valued at $50.00. $50,000 in 45 days – not bad money). The trapper gets $9.00 for every hide he brings in. The company takes the rest.

I am sleepy, so I'll write some more tomorrow. Pleasant dreams. Our time is 3 hours later than yours. It is now 11:00 here and I am with you.

Royse

Kanaga Island, Territory of Alaska   Tuesday, 2 Nov 1937

My dearest Babe,

Today has been something like yesterday. Musick and me went for a walk over the hills. Saw an eagle, found some moonstones and sponges. I don't know how sponges ever come to be up here. Found a pile of driftwood at the mouth of a stream. Some pretty good size logs, too. They must have come a long way, as there are no trees on this island.

The volcano looks pretty. Its sides are covered with snow. Some of the men said they saw smoke coming from the top, but I doubt it. This island consists of hills and valleys. Every valley has a lake or stream. Sometimes both. Mr. Kellerman went fishing. He caught quite a mess of fish – all small trouts. I may go sometime. There's a flock of little sea birds here that resemble snipes. May try to trap them sometime.

Royse

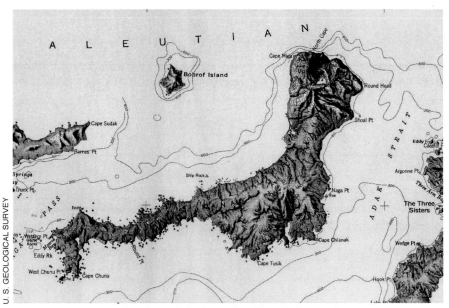

Kanaga Island, with hills and valleys, lakes and streams

Kanaga Island, Territory of Alaska   Thursday, 4 Nov 1937

Dear Babe & Babies,

Last evening Mr. Kellerman had a party for some of his officer friends and the caretaker and his wife. Musick cooked, I waited on the table. I wore blue trousers, white shirt & tie and have whiskers that are two weeks old. Some sight. We put out a pretty nice dinner, even if all of it was from cans.

Today has been a little different. Musick and me took a fishing rod & a rifle. We tramped over about three miles of swamps and hills, looking for something to shoot at or a hole for fish. Musick caught a fish about four inches long and shot an eagle that has a wingspread of over six feet.

The hills are covered with coarse grass & moss. When I step on it I sink in a few inches. That makes it very tiresome for walking. And, too, the boots I have are two sizes too big for me. We got them big so we could have two pairs of woolen socks on at one time.

The trappers are moving in now. They are a dirty-looking bunch. Two or three of them live next door to us. They resemble Japanese very much. One of them is a hunchback. There is one nitwit of a white boy in the outfit.

You know, in Annapolis we often talked of scraping the bear c. off the front porch. Well, the little foxes actually get up on the doorstep and dirty on it. Nearly everywhere we step we get our shoes dirty. If our clothes blow off the line at night the fox will get up on the middle of the garment and c. right in the middle of it. Nice fox. No more tonight. Pleasant dreams.

Royse

Kanaga Island, Territory of Alaska   Friday, 5 Nov 1937

Dear Babe,

Well, another day has passed. We measured Musick's eagle today. 7 ft from tip to tip of each wing. He really was a big one.

Nothing of any special interest occurred today, although it seems that everything has gone wrong. Have one man on the sick list. He has a cold.

The people here have a herd of goats. About the 15th of January I will be the milk man for them. The Clarks (Mr. & Mrs.) are leaving about then and they won't need the milk — so we get it — if we want it. Perhaps I can talk these people out of one of the kids — would rather have a dog, though.

Today we have had snow, rain, sleet, sunshine, rainbows, and wind. One part of the place where we live may be perfectly calm, while a few hundred yards away a stiff breeze will be blowing.

The radio station and weather station are set up and are to be in working order tonight. The Tanager will leave tomorrow, so that leaves us all alone for the Winter. We will be pretty busy until sometime in December. The station ship which is in here will make a trip to Dutch Harbor sometime before X-mas. We will get mail then and again sometime in March. So until then I will say Good Night and Pleasant Dreams.

                                        Royse

Among several photos taken and developed by the men on Kanaga Island in the winter of 1937–38 was this one, probably of Clyde Musick with the eagle he shot.

Kanaga Island, Territory of Alaska   Friday, 5 Nov 1937

SPECIAL LETTER JUST TO ROYSE'S CHILDREN Ellen & Estelle

My Babies:

You have been in bed for over three hours now. For I am farther away from you than Honolulu. So the difference in time is three hours. When it is sundown with you, it is only afternoon here.

When I got up this morning there was snow on the ground. Won't be long until Santa Claus comes. There are some reindeer on the other island. I wonder if they belong to Santa Claus. When he comes by here I will give him your list of things. I really think he should bring you some Eskimo boots and an Eskimo ball, too.

Now about your school work. Are you doing your lessons as you should? I think daddy's girls are doing all right. You may get lazy sometimes, but all in all I will bet you can work real good now.

How about the garden you put in – did you get any peas and beans from it? We will put in a good one next time.

Did I tell you about the baby goats here? Well, they have two baby goats. They are black. Poppy will milk the mammy goat pretty soon, so we can have milk with our cornflakes.

Now this eagle we killed – he was a big bird. He could carry Ivarene's baby off. The eagles kill and eat the foxes. They eat the fish, too.* One of the men saw a seal on the rocks last week. I want to shoot one so we can have his skin for a rug.

Lots of foxes live under our house. They are real pretty. The people catch them in traps to get their fur or skin. They are a dark blue color.

---

*Despite the fact that the bald eagle had been the U. S. national bird since the 1780s, in 1917 it was considered a scourge in Alaska. The Alaska Territorial Legislature instituted a bounty that lasted until 1952.

Ellen, that was a nice letter you sent to me. I like to get your letters. Estelle, you write some, too.

Do you girls like your teachers? I think you will like school better after Christmas. If you could be up here, you would not have to go to school. You would almost freeze, though, because it is cold and windy.

Nearly every morning I wake up thinking about my girls. I wonder if they are in school and if they eat their food like they should and if they brush their teeth. I suppose that Santa Claus will tell me about it when he comes by. He will go from here to Honolulu, because Honolulu is closer. I know he will tell me you are good girls, because he knows I love both of you.

Poppy

Kanaga Diary

After the last mail boat of the season left Kanaga Island, probably on November 5, Royse Gibson continued to write his letters, in the form of a diary of his day-to-day thoughts and activities, keeping alive his sense of connection with his wife and daughters in San Diego. He begins with a summary of his trip north on the USS *Portland*, some of which he had also described in the letters he wrote and mailed home earlier.

On Kanaga the men who were monitoring radio communications and recording weather data had their daily work cut out for them. The work of Musick the cook, though routine, was well defined and essential to the functioning of the station. In contrast, with such a small population and because it was rare that anyone got sick or hurt, Royse Gibson, the medic, had very little to do. The commanding officer, Lt. Kellerman, oversaw the activities of the seven men.

All eight of the men stationed at Kanaga Island that winter had to contend with isolation and a very limited list of things to do in their free time. But for Gibson the passing of time would have been especially slow, and the days particularly monotonous.

Sunday, 14 Nov 1937 on Kanaga Island

My dearest Ione & Babies:

This letter will be in the form of a diary. I don't know when mail will go out. The ship which is stationed here — the Dorothea (a company ship) — makes an occasional trip to Dutch Harbor, but has no regular schedule. I'll send it when I can. You should have a letter which I sent out on the Tanager on the 5th. The radioman at Dutch Harbor says that we have lots of mail. Of course there may be some for me, too. We landed here three weeks ago today. It seems much longer, because I count my time from the 3rd of October.

Now to tell you about this place. I must begin from the time I left you — or you left me, because I was standing still when you drove away. Well, after you left I went up on the deck, where I met CPhM Day from the Pennsylvania. He talked awhile about this trip and of Masley. Then I caught a Northampton boat. When I got on board her I was immediately transferred to the Portland for some reason.

On the Portland I met Dr. Robertson from Annapolis again. Gage & Harrell have left her for other parts. Dr. Robertson was very glad to see me, because he thought I was to remain on the Portland.

We left San Pedro after a few days' stay as you know. The trip up to Bremerton was pleasant. We didn't see much of the coast until we got right into the harbor. The weather was foggy most of the way, too.

I like the Bremerton country. Lots of timber. Plenty of water, too. I believe you would like it also. Maybe something like Annapolis. So perhaps I had better be cautious about liking it.

We got to Bremerton on Sunday, I think. At any rate, the next day I met three more of the men who are in the party. The Captain called us in and asked where we were going and who was in charge. We knew nothing at all.

Well, we started to fitting out. This is a partial list of the things we got: clothing, rubber boots, shoe pacs (Arctic shoes), rainproof clothing, windproof clothing, sheepskin-lined coats, heavy underwear, woolen socks, submarine coats & trousers, and a few other items. I, of course, had to get my medicines, which took two days, and then after that we had to get our groceries – about $2,200 worth.

There are eight of us in this party. Lieut. Kellerman from New Mexico in charge; Cunningham, ACRM* from Montana; Cowell, CAerM** from North Dakota; myself; Erwin, AerM3c*** from Arkansas; Rodman, ARM3c† from New York; Musick, SClc†† from Texas; and Southerland, Slc††† from South Carolina. Three Chiefs, one First Class, two Third Class, one Seaman, and a Lieutenant in the party.

Well, we got our supplies and other stuff on board. There were 20 tons of coal, 130 drums of fuel oil & gasoline, besides tons of radio and other equipment. Southerland was transferred across country by plane to catch the Portland.

We left Bremerton around 3 PM Friday. Had fine weather for two days, then the storm broke. The oil was stored aft on the stern of the ship. It got loose and began to bounce around. We lost about 35 barrels of it.

---

*ACRM is *Aviation Chief Radioman.*
**CAerM is *Chief Aerographer's Mate.*
***AerM3c is *Aerographer's Mate 3rd Class.*
†ARM3c is *Aviation Radioman 3rd Class.*
††SClc is *Ship's Cook 1st Class.*
†††Slc is *Seaman 1st Class.*

We got to Dutch Harbor on the first stop. Stayed there two days. I went ashore one evening just to take a look at the place. Dr. Robertson went over to see the Public Health Hospital. He was nice and impressed with it.

We left Dutch Harbor one afternoon and got in here Sunday morning. At 1300 (1 PM) we disembarked, all eight of us. The Portland sent over a working party of 15 men to help us to get established. My medical supplies came in two boxes and, as usual, there is everything except what is likely to be needed most. Well, so far there has been no need for anything.

After we got here and got our personal stuff on the dock we took a look and here is what we saw and had to work with: First, this island is about 26 miles long by 14 or 15 miles wide. There is a volcano on the northeast end of it. The land is very hilly, has lots of small streams and lakes. There is a very good harbor here at the station. The hills are all covered with tundra grass and moss. The moss has a little berry on it like the Ohelo berry at the Hilo volcano.

The island has been stocked with blue foxes (supposed to be about 2000 of them). No rats, frogs, or other animal life. A good many eagles, however.

A long building serves as a store, warehouse, and living quarters for the caretaker & his wife. There is another large two-story storehouse here and a chicken house, barn, and two cabins (trappers' cabins). This place is a community in itself. There is a light power plant, oil furnace for heating, blacksmith shop, carpenter shop, and a workshop where nearly any kind of work can be done. There is also a dock about 150 ft long. We have modern plumbing and lighting.

Well, after taking care of ourselves we started to work uncrating our stores. That took about two weeks. The Portland left us on Thursday (28 October). We had two yard employees and a lieutenant who were here to install the radio apparatus. My job was and is houseboy and mess cook. I have had two cut fingers to take care of so far. Also a case of itch on the foot and a sprained ankle.

Wednesday, 24 Nov 1937 on Kanaga Island

Still writing. After the Portland left, the Lieut & two civilians stayed here for another week to finish the radio installation. The Tanager stayed in here to assist and to take the above three back to Dutch Harbor. Bricker is on the Tanager. After the Tanager left, we were left all alone.

We started having only two meals a day – breakfast at 0900, no dinner, and supper at 1700 (5 PM), and we don't get so hungry after all. We drink lots of coffee, of course. There are always two pots on the stove.

Thursday, 25 Nov 1937 on Kanaga Island

Thanksgiving Day. Well, today has been very quiet. Had a little special dinner today. Pot roast of beef, onions, potatoes, carrots, mince pie, candy, fruit (oranges & apples), olives, mixed pickles, and cocoa.

I believe I have told you about all there is about getting off the ship, unpacking, getting set up, etc. The aerological part has instruments for recording the wind velocity and direction, the temperature of the air and of the sea water, the amount of rain, snow, sunshine, and even the height and type of clouds. And all this stuff is recorded hourly, too.

When I got up this morning there was snow on the ground – looks like a White Christmas. A couple of weeks ago Musick killed an eagle. Cowell killed one a few days later. I shot six plover yesterday. That is all that I've killed. Mr. Kellerman & I went fishing once, caught a few trout that were full of worms. Shot two salmon – full of worms, too. The salmon come into fresh water to lay their eggs and then die. They seem to just rot and decay away. These streams here are full of salmon now.

I am writing this in bed. There is no hurry to finish, because mail doesn't leave until March sometime.

Friday, 26 Nov 1937 on Kanaga Island

Well, today Musick tried to bake bread, without much success. The yeast must be old, because he certainly tried to bake it. He got discouraged and left me to finish supper while he went goose hunting. He got wet to the skin and the geese got away.

This week we painted the kitchen white. Tonight we trimmed the place in a Nile green. I think it looks good. The deck has been oiled and is, or was, filthy. We scrubbed it off with lye and now it is really white. Have two more rooms to paint.

Saturday, 27 Nov 1937 on Kanaga Island

The lights went out last night, so I wrote the last three words in darkness. Well, today we fiddled around. I refitted the door on the toilet. Musick finished the trimming in green and baked bread.

It is now about ten o'clock, or two o'clock in San Diego. We are thirty minutes past Honolulu and four hours behind you. So you and our Babies have been asleep for four or five hours, I hope. The lights are going out again, soon.

This morning I took a shot at an eagle. As usual I missed him. Sometime I will make a mistake and get one. There are lots of ravens here, too. Musick killed one with a shotgun not so long ago.

I've patched one pair of drawers, dungarees, and a shirt so far. Have another shirt to go and one pair of drawers, too. Wish we had a sewing machine. We have the privilege of using the electric washing machine. Mrs. Clark (the caretaker's wife) assigned us to Thursday and Friday for washing. Now she wants it to be Wednesday and Thursday. She is nutty, anyway. I am going to sleep. Pleasant dreams.

Monday, 29 Nov 1937 on Kanaga Island

Dear Babe:

We painted the heads and living room today. Finished the heads and have one more coat to put on the living room.

We are having lots of wind and some snow now. The snow melts in the low places. The hilltops are covered all the time. All the trappers are out now. They will begin trapping in about two weeks. I certainly do wish I could get you two fox furs. Can get the furs for $10 each, but can not get them made up, because they are not registered (bootleg furs).

Yesterday Mr. Kellerman killed an eagle. It was a young one. I am saving the wing and tail feathers of all of them. Will send them to some Indian Chief or let the Babies have them if they want them.

Now about my whiskers. I have not shaved for five weeks. You should see the Santa Claus face I have. No more for tonight. The Dorothea leaves here about the 10th of February, so will probably get this out on it.

Wednesday, 1 Dec 1937 on Kanaga Island

Dear Munner:

A few more lines tonight. We had an earthquake this morning about breakfast time. Just one shake and that was all.

Today we finished the painting. Have to clean the deck up now and paint in the angle iron. Will do that tomorrow.

Today is the Clarks' 20th wedding anniversary. They are not on speaking terms yet. I really feel sorry for her. She is here all by herself. Never gets out of the house except to dust out the rug. He (Clark) is somewhat of a louse. Oh well!

They killed a fox today. Their fur is nice. Most of it is in the tail. Will begin trapping in earnest about the 15th of this month. This place has a pen for the foxes. The trappers have about a dozen of them penned up, just keeping them until cold weather sets in.

Mr. Kellerman went on a goose hunt this afternoon. Was up on them, but they got away again. He certainly has bad luck with his hunting. Musick and me will go out for a couple of hours tomorrow. I really want to shoot an eagle. No more news tonight.

Thursday, 2 Dec 1937 on Kanaga Island

Well, we scrubbed the deck down with lye water today, but did not finish putting the paint on. Will tomorrow, I suppose. Mr. Kellerman and me went out on a grave-robbing expedition. We found a few pieces of bone and that is all. There is an old burial ground out on a point here where the natives years ago buried their dead. So we went out to open a grave. I would be unlucky enough to dig right between two graves anyway. Perhaps we will try again sometime.*

The weather has been bad all day – wind and rain, off and on all day. We can have greater varieties of wind here than any one place that I have ever been.

Was talking to Musick about farms around Seattle. He says that land there is dirt cheap right now. We could get this place pretty cheap, too – if you would care to live here 212 miles from the nearest neighbor. Would you like it? I really would, I believe.

No more to tell you tonight. Wonder if you ever got the pictures and if the proof that I have isn't the best one. I suppose the other proofs are in Dutch Harbor.

---

*At the time, digging for bones and artifacts in Aleut burials and abandoned dwellings was commonplace. Sometimes the diggers sought souvenirs to keep, sometimes to sell to private buyers or museums. In 1979 the Archeological Resources Protection Act and in 1990 the Native American Graves Protection and Repatriation Act established rules for excavating or collecting Native American human remains or cultural items and procedures for their repatriation, and also made it a criminal offense to traffic in these items without right of possession.

Friday, 3 Dec 1937 on Kanaga Island

Well, today has been a little different. We painted the baseboards and finished all the painting, as far as I am concerned.

Musick and me went out grave robbing. I found two or three stone lamps and stone axes. Musick found almost a complete skeleton, and two arrowheads, one of stone and one of bone — also a bone spear point. This place where I dug I found a flat stone which covered a hole about 3 ft deep and about a foot across. There was nothing in the hole. The floors of these huts are covered with shells and fish bones. Strange — it almost seems like they threw the refuse on the deck and lived on top of it. We will try again tomorrow if nothing happens.

Tonight we had Swiss steak. Seems like all we do is eat, clean up, sweep, and then begin the next meal. I have just finished sewing a pair of trousers. You should see the job. Have one leg longer than the other. Well, I expected that.

Not so long until Christmas. I've been thinking of the Eldrices all day. Wonder why? Have been thinking a lot about my girls, too. Hope they are good girls. I think they are. Sometimes they might be a little naughty. Most of the time they are good and always intend to be good girls.

<u>Saturday 4 Dec 1937 on Kanaga Island</u>

This morning Musick and me cleaned up early and went back to our diggings. This is a description of the place: The people lived in huts made of sod and driftwood. This hut we are working in looks like this:

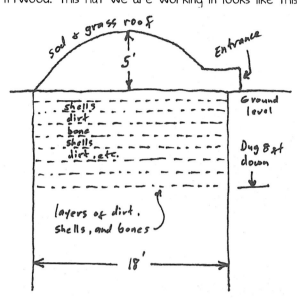

They seemed to have dug a well about 18 ft across and lived in it. There are layers of fish, bird, and other bones all the way down. I dug down for about 8 ft and still found more layers of seashells and fish and bird bones. This is the place where Musick found the human skeleton and arrowheads. I want to dig this place out complete, just to see how it was made. Seems that they lived in these places, slept, cooked, and ate in them. All the refuse they threw on the deck, then covered it with a layer of clean dirt and lived on top of that until they needed another layer of dirt, and so on. Now, whether they built the house up as it filled up or if they dug it deep to begin with I do not know. I found a stone scraper today. Musick got three scrapers and a spear point (bone). Also a stone lamp or cook pot. I want to dig to the bottom, while he wants souvenirs. I'll get mine later.

Monday, 6 Dec 1937 on Kanaga Island

Saturday Mr. Kellerman and Erwin went goose-hunting. They shot five or six but only got home with four. Musick & me picked the breast feathers out of them for the Lieutenant's pillow, then hung them up on the back porch of the house to air out. They smell like a sardine from too many fish. Am writing this page over because there was some part of it you might not like if I am not there to grin while you read it.

Sunday afternoon Mr. Kellerman and I went out to our diggings. On the way out he killed a duck. I took the gizzard out and we left the carcass on the bank to be picked up when we came back. The crows beat us to it. So we shot a crow. We found a stone lamp, stone adze, and a cook pot in the hut.

This morning Musick & me went out. I found a bone awl and a stone scraper. We found another village to dig in. On the way over we saw a flock of five ptarmigan. I shot four of them. Musick shot one with a rifle. Mr. Kellerman killed an eagle today, too. Rodman & Erwin killed three ducks and a crow. Am still hoping for a seal. The skin is not good for anything except for a rug or something like that.

Have really been homesick for the last two days. Can't afford to have that feeling. You can't get homesick because you are home. Perhaps you sometimes wish to see me. I will request to be relieved in March. If I am relieved then, it will be the first of May before I get back to San Diego. If there is no relief then it will be about the first of November before I can get back. May have to find a new family then. Will stop the allotment and find where you are.

Yes, and too, all allotments stop the first of March. So be sure to check on the Bremerton bank to pay the Pittsburgh Insurance if there is not enough in Vallejo. Dreamed a few nights ago that you had sold the car — now have you? Pleasant dreams.

<u>Wednesday, 8 Dec 1937 on Kanaga Island</u>

Got up about 8 AM. Not a cloud in sight. Today has really been a beautiful day. Cunningham & Southerland went fishing this morning. They got 7 or 8 codfish and one halibut. Mr. Kellerman went on a hunting trip — didn't even take a shot at anything. Musick & me stayed home and baked bread. He is doing pretty good with his baking now. I cleaned house all morning. Washed our clothes, sorted out the carrots, and fiddled around the rest of the day.

For supper we had corned beef, cabbage, carrots, potatoes, hot buns, jam, honey, and cup custard. Does that sound good to you? Mr. Kellerman is talking of bringing his wife & baby (7-yr-old girl) up here. I would like for you & my girls to come up here. It just isn't worth it, however. If we could leave the girls with someone (which is out of the question) and you came alone — I am certain you would enjoy this place. Don't be surprised if I send for you, but at the same time do not make any preparations, because I doubt if I could get transportation for dependents. It just would not be right to take the babies out of school and bring them way up here to freeze. So all this is just another pipe dream.

Yesterday I went grave digging. Found a bone spearhead and two or three other things. Also a walrus or some kind of tooth. Oh yes, last night we had roast goose for supper. It didn't go over so good as it was too fishy and had the "wild game" taste. Will have fish tomorrow night.

The herd of goats (about 14 of them) came in today. From the way they look I will have to start milking before the first of the year. Just wonder if it would be possible to palm off a goat skin on you for a seal skin.

The volcano certainly looked pretty today. Not a cloud over it and just a haze of smoke at the peak. The peak is about 15 miles away but only looks to be about five miles. To look at it through binoculars it seems to be just a few yards.

Will have to give in and love you just a little tonight. I don't want to, because it makes me homesick and there is no use of that. At the same time I wonder how you feel about being loved. Wonder if you would not like for me to have you in my arms. Do you miss having me tease you? Are you enjoying a rest? Maybe the girls are not learning any cussing in the house now and no one is pinching you or doing things which they should not. One thing certain – I am not teaching them any naughty sayings. It's bedtime. Pleasant dreams to all.

Thursday, 9 Dec 1937 on Kanaga Island

Today has been windy, cold, and wet. I have not done a thing worthwhile. Just cleaned up this morning and read the rest of the day. As usual, will do it all tomorrow. Did sew a rip in my rainproof trousers and patched something else. I do not remember what it was now. Dreamed last night that I had G.C.* Wonder why I dream these things? Was certainly glad to wake up.

The trappers killed a fox today. They are pretty animals. I do not believe it possible to tame them. The people say they are excellent ratters. Must be, because there are no rats on this island. The owners have tried to raise rabbits, but they did not last long. The foxes got

---

*G.C. is gonorrhea.

them all. Between the eagles, crows, and foxes, the rabbits would have a hard time.

We had fried fresh halibut for supper. It really was good. I do wish you could have had some of it. Tomorrow we will have ptarmigan, and Saturday we will have baked codfish. Musick and me are called Colonel just like a Kentucky "Kunnel, Suh". We have made Cowell a stable sergeant, because he has a horsey smell.

The radio weather reports are that all the coast is having severe storms and plenty of rain. Wonder if I will ever see San Diego when it is really green. Am too sleepy to write any more, so will say good night again and pleasant dreams. Would certainly like to hear my baby say, "See you in the morning."

Friday, 10 Dec 1937 on Kanaga Island

Well, today has not been so much. Had breakfast and went out to dump the garbage. Took a rifle along. Did not see a thing to shoot at. Took a walk along the beach, looking for glass balls, which the Japanese use for floats on their fishing nets. Did not find any. I have four already. Will have a basket full before long.

Glass floats that had broken free from Japanese fishing nets often washed up on beaches in the Aleutian Islands and in the Pacific Northwest.

PHOTO: JONATHAN ZANDER

As you have noticed, I have not sent you any radio messages. This station is more or less secret and not many messages go out. And another thing, the radioman and me do not get along so well. So you are not getting many communications. Also, if I do send you a message, it will go from here to Dutch Harbor via radio, and then to Seattle by cable, and then from Seattle to San Diego via Western Union, and it would cost about 20 cents per word from Dutch Harbor on. I do not have that much to say.

Tonight we had ptarmigan for supper. I really liked it. Had a wild taste, but after all, that is what makes game so prized as food.

Would like to visit with you tonight. Lots of things to tell you and lots more questions to ask. I suppose the Gamble has been placed in "red-lead-row" for dismantling a long time ago, and that the crew has been distributed to all points of the compass by this time.* Have one object left now – just to get the next two years in and quit. What do you think?

Tonight after supper I read awhile and then sewed a binding on a floor mat for the hallway. You really should see the homeward stitches I took in the canvas bindings at each end. Last night I started to patch my underwear. Couldn't find my patching materials, so I went to bed. Pleasant Dreams.

Poppy

---

*USS Gamble was a destroyer in the U. S. Navy during World War I. Royse Gibson had served on the ship at some point later. Far from being decommissioned, the *Gamble* was converted to a minelayer and served in World War II, earning seven battle stars for service before being damaged beyond repair. It was decommissioned and intentionally sunk off Guam.

<u>Saturday, 11 Dec 1937 on Kanaga Island</u>

Dear Mommy and Girls:

Last night we had snow. All the hills are white. Looks very much like a White Christmas. This morning Mr. Kellerman and me went out hunting. We did not kill a thing until we started home. Shot 8 little snipes. Could only get six of them – the other two were out in the water in the rocks.

Today the trappers killed all the foxes that they had penned up here at the house. We will take the carcasses and stake them out so we can use them for eagle bait. I'll kill an eagle yet.

The temperature tonight is 28 degrees F. That is only 4 degrees below freezing. Was 22 degrees below zero the lowest we had at Annapolis? I sometimes believe it was colder than that.

Dreamed about Mooney a few nights ago. He & I were in some kind of a scrape. No more to tell you. Good night and pleasant dreams.

<u>Sunday, 12 Dec 1937 on Kanaga Island</u>

Another day has passed. This morning we carried 11 bags (1100 lbs) of coal. I got five bags of it. This afternoon Mr. Kellerman and me went out on a crow-shooting trip. We both shot at a crow and down he came with a broken wing. I went over and twisted his head off. They are very tough critters. We have all the foxes staked out for eagle bait. Hope we get one or two.

Well, the Asiatic Menace looks bad. I hope that I've left you fixed the best I can, and you remember what I've told you about taking care of yourself. Let us hope that all this will blow over. However, I am afraid it won't. Tonight I scrubbed all my clothes, including a heavy canvas jacket. It was worse than a sea bag to clean and believe me, it was dirty. Was full of grease and coal dust.

Got your picture out today (the proof of you and me). You look just as good to me as ever. Will bet that the proofs of the girls are in Dutch Harbor. We may get mail in January. Pleasant dreams.

Monday, 13 Dec 1937 on Kanaga Island

This morning Southerland and me took the boat & outboard motor & went fishing. We caught a big double-ugly fish and a codfish. Neither fish was fit for food. The codfish had worms in it. A wind came up which began to take us out to sea. The motor would not run, so we began rowing back. I was glad to get back inside of the harbor.

This evening all hands went skiing and out coasting on a toboggan sled. I have not tried either. Am getting too old for such foolishness.

A sculpin known locally in Alaska as the double-ugly fish is also known as the Irish lord.

According to radio reports tonight Japan has said that she is sorry for bombing our ships.* So all is forgiven. Well, that sounds nice.

The temperature at 7:00 PM (11:00 PM your time) was 20 degrees. No wind. The hills are covered with snow. The country is really beautiful. Musick killed two crows today. I'll try my luck tomorrow.

Do you really want to come up here? It is nice to dream about it, but there really is no place for you. Just another daydream. It's time to go to bed. And do some real dreaming. Good night to all my girls – all three of you.

---

*Reference here is to the "Panay Incident," when Japanese bombers attacked American and British ships near Nanking, China on December 12, 1937. Nanking fell to the Japanese the next day. Historians claim the bombing of the Panay, an American gunboat, was intentional, but the American public accepted the Japanese apologies for the accident that were offered at the time.

PHOTO: U. S. GOVERNMENT

The USS Panay *sinks after bombing by Japanese planes.*

Tuesday, 14 Dec 1937 on Kanaga Island

Another day has just about passed. All that I have done today has been to scrape the paint off the toilet seat and read. Think of it – I have read a whole book of 400 pages. The first one in months, I believe.

Today has been real nice. All the men except me went skiing. I may try it sometime. Seems that I want to be alone, so I stay alone. You know me pretty well, so you understand that I like to be by myself at times.

Wonder what the fleet is doing at this time. I would say that it is preparing in a big way. From radio reports the whole affair looks pretty bad. Well, I do not see what we on Kanaga can do.

Also see where California is having lots of rain. Has it washed any part of Island Avenue away? Had a little snow tonight. The moon is doing its best to shine through the clouds. I wonder if you look at the moon sometimes and wonder if I, too, am seeing the same moon and thinking of you. I really wonder if you sometimes do. Good night.

Wednesday, 15 Dec 1937 on Kanaga Island

Today has been very quiet. I have only been out of the house once. Patched a pair of drawers tonight and typed a page for Mr. Kellerman. Have had the blues all day. I feel that you, too, have been moody. Several times I have counted on my fingers the days until I can leave here. Also the days until mail leaves and until it gets here.

From the way the news broadcast sounded, the Japanese are quite perturbed about the "Panay" affair. I suppose they are "So Sorry" about it. A few more weeks will tell the story. I do so hope the U. S. A. can hold off for a year or so at least.

Just two months ago today we left Seattle (Bremerton). Doesn't seem so long ago. Would like to bring you and the babes up here. Am afraid that you would not like it and also it would mean loss of a lot of schooling for our girlies. Oh well, if Christmas comes, March can not be so far away.

The same old story – no more news, so I'll go to sleep. Good night to all. I'll see you in the morning – or let us say tomorrow evening.

Thursday, 16 Dec 1937 on Kanaga Island

We inventoried our groceries today. So far we have lived for about $26 per month per man. Now, if we can live like that the rest of the months we are here, we (you and I) should have a little money ahead. The total cost of the food for each man is about $255, which will be paid for by the 15th of April. After that the bank account should go up fast. I think we should have close to $500 for ourselves when I get back. How are you doing? I have not spent a nickel since the first of November. Have you done as well?

Don't fail to give your shoe sizes and other information in the next letter. Will get all of you some boots on the way back.

Today has been about the same old story. Up at 7:30, breakfast at 9 o'clock, clean up and get supper ready. You know we only eat twice a day now.

Tonight I made a shelf for the dishpan and darned a pair of socks. Also washed all my clothes. Would you like to be loved a little tonight?

I would. How about my girls — would they like to have a goodnight mootsie? Best of luck to all of you, and pleasant dreams. I'll see you tomorrow night.

Royse

<u>Saturday, 18 Dec 1937 on Kanaga Island</u>

Dearest Mommy & babies,

I missed last night because I was doing some typing for Mr. Kellerman — and I wanted to finish reading a book.

Well, yesterday was just another day. I went out on a shooting trip and did not shoot a thing. Well, I did cripple a water fowl and he got away to lie among the rocks somewhere. And I found a burial place, too. Found some bones in it. Today Musick and me went out to the burial mound and dug it out. Am too sleepy tonight to tell you all the details, so I'll go to sleep and tell you everything next time. Pleasant dreams to all.

Sunday, 19 Dec 1937 on Kanaga Island

Dear Girls (the three of you),

    Friday we did about the usual things. I went out with the shotgun. Shot a water bird as I told you. On the way home I took a look into a hole which I thought was a fox hole. I saw some bones in it. So on Saturday Musick, Mr. Kellerman, and I went over and dug it out. It was an Aleut grave, but someone else had beat us to it. All the bones were there except the skull. There were no arrowheads or stone implements. Now every little hummock we see we dig up, and it never amounts to a thing.

    Today (Sunday) Musick and I had pancakes for breakfast. We cleaned up and scrubbed the decks with hot soapy water, then went on an eagle hunt. He shot one and I put four shots into the back of another one with a shot gun. He was too far away to do any good. This eagle that Musick shot fell into the water and drifted out to sea, so we lost him. Mr. Kellerman went on a goose hunt and got one goose. Musick and me may go out tomorrow morning early.

    Tonight we had canned chicken ravioli for supper. Will have ham omelette for breakfast. The company ship is leaving now about 11:45 PM for a trip to all the islands to pick up the trappers. There is no more to tell you tonight, so I will go to sleep. The days are slipping by pretty fast now. We are all living and planning until March, when the mail comes in – just about two months away. Pleasant dreams to all.

Monday, 20 Dec 1937 on Kanaga Island

Well, today has been a long one. Got up early – went out to the fox carcasses to look for an eagle, but there were none in sight. Had breakfast and then went out hunting geese. They got away before we could get a shot at them.

All the hills are covered with snow yet, so we are having a White Christmas. Finished the typing for Mr. Kellerman tonight. I will keep pecking on the machine so I will be able to get an office job when I am through up here. You know, as I think about it, I think you should come up here for a while. What do you think? Well, it is almost midnight, so I must say "Good Night and Pleasant Dreams" again.

Tuesday, 21 Dec 1937 on Kanaga Island

Dear Ones:

Today has been bad. Started raining last night and has kept it up all day. The snow has just about all gone now. I suppose the White Christmas has gone, too.

All of our outfit has reached the point where none of us speak to each other, and we have only been here two months. Such a life. Have not done a thing today to tell you about. The company ship which is stationed here, "Dorothea," came in today. You know she went out Sunday night to pick up some trappers on other islands. The sea was too rough to make a landing, so she came back without picking anybody up.

I think they will leave here for Seattle about the first of February. Mrs. Clark, the manager's wife, is packing, preparatory to leaving. Good night & pleasant dreams.

Wednesday, 22 Dec 1937 on Kanaga Island

Dearest girls,

Today has been about the same as yesterday. The snow is just about all gone now. We washed the windows today – a grand clean-up for the holiday. We hear the radio broadcasts from Seattle, San Diego, Los Angeles, Salt Lake City, and Honolulu. Did not hear the news tonight nor last night. Seems like there is less to tell you each night.

Some of the trappers are coming in. The catch of foxes is very small this year. I have the fox skin fever – fifty dollars for one skin is just more than we can afford, isn't it? Wonder if Flemings will have anything for Christmas now after the Anniversary presents? Was about this time or a little later a few years ago that I made a fast trip to see you, wasn't it? I am certainly glad that I am not on the destroyers that went to sea so suddenly and secretly. Again, pleasant dreams.

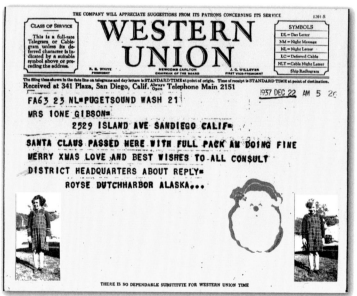

A Christmas radiogram from Royse to his family. Ione added the Santa and the photos of Ellen (left) and Estelle.

Thursday, 23 Dec 1937 on Kanaga Island

This morning I washed about all the clothes that I own. We have the use of a washing machine. I put them all on to boil last night – and then boiled them again this morning. They are really clean.

We have had rain and wind all day. This afternoon Musick, Mr. Kellerman, and I went on a goose-trapping expedition. We have a net, box trap, and steel traps. Surely we'll get something.

Tonight we just sat around and talked. I have just finished another book, "Pearl Diver." It is a pretty good book of adventure. Mrs. Clark has a very pretty Christmas Tree. An artificial tree such as you wanted to keep and I wanted to throw away. Christmas for her is going to be very dull, and I wonder about you.

We start to baking tomorrow. Will have a little extra chow, I suppose. Nothing new, as usual. Good night.

Friday, 24 Dec 1937 on Kanaga Island

My dearest Ione and Babies:

Today has been a better day. This morning I was up at 0700. Mr. Kellerman and I went up to the traps. I shot three geese and did not get a one of them. Just crippled them. Mr. Kellerman had a goose in his trap. We brought him in and dried him out. He was almost drowned. I had to cut one of his toes off – it was broken.

When I got back, your radio was here. All I've done today is read. Have not been out of the house much. Finished reading "Pearl Diver." I think the boat is going to Dutch Harbor soon. Hope to get a few letters if she does.

Yesterday Musick left the skiff on the far side of the bay. I rowed it back and let me tell you, it was a job. The tide and wind were against me. I made it after almost pulling my arms off.

If you get this letter before 5 March, will you send an order to Sears Roebuck in Seattle for 2 dungaree shirts, size 16, 35-inch sleeve, and 2 pr dungaree pants, Size 34-34. Not over 75 cents each for the shirts and about $1.00 each for the pants.

And another thing: How do you feel about coming up here? We would be as broke as ever if you do and it will mean taking our girls out of school. You would really enjoy being here, though. I am not even certain that I can get transportation for you. As before, it makes a nice daydream. Must say good night, pleasant dreams, and wish you a pleasant Christmas.

Saturday, 25 Dec 1937 – Christmas day on Kanaga Island

Would it mean much to wish you a Merry Christmas? Our dinner is over. We had a pretty good chow after all. Went out on the goose trap line but didn't catch a thing. Ah, to hell with what we did today. I want to see you and our babies. I certainly would like to be with you now. Almost three months since I left San Diego. I suppose my little girls are growing up and I am certain they are nice girls and are doing their lessons nice. Now about their mother. I would like to see her, too. And just wonder what she is doing tonight. Right now I am certain all of you are in bed fast asleep and that is what I am going to do right now, so pleasant dreams to all of you.

Royse

Sunday, 26 Dec 1937 on Kanaga Island

Mrs. Clark gave all of us a handkerchief apiece for Christmas, which is very nice of her. Today has been a real nice day. As usual I stayed in all day. Well, I did get out for about two hours. Was fishing for a while. Had a big fish on the hook, and as usual he got away. Finally managed to bring a piece of metal up. Rowed across the bay to scare some geese into the traps. The homesickness still has me. I certainly do want to be with all of you. Will just have to get over it.

The boat is bringing the furs in. White foxes sell for $17 each, while blues are $40 to $90 per skin. Do you want any of them? One of the men saw 12 seals in the bay a few days ago. I really do want to get a seal skin. Tomorrow Musick and I want to go across to Skull Bay on another bone hunt. Before then I think I'll read your letters over. Good Night.

Monday, 27 Dec 1937 on Kanaga Island

This month is near an end, isn't it? Wasn't it about nine years ago that I made a trip to San Diego to see you? Wonder if you would be as glad to see me now. This morning three of us went across the bay to dig in a few more graves. Didn't find anything. I want to try again sometime, I am certain that I can find a skull somewhere. Did dig out a few teeth.

Tonight is cold and windy. I certainly did want to be with you this evening. And still want to. Nothing out of the ordinary has happened today. I may as well go to sleep. Again I say good night and pleasant dreams to all.

<u>Tuesday, 28 Dec 1937 on Kanaga Island</u>

Today has been a little different from the other days. Woke up this morning and the wind and rain were strong. Went out for a goose and we had one in the traps. Have two here, now. It has been cold and foggy all day. I tried fishing awhile this afternoon and had the usual luck – nothing. Stayed in all day. Well, I did take a look at the goose's foot – had to cut one toe off, because it was broken in the trap.

Have read a lot today and spent a lot of time day-dreaming about the future. I would like to have a shore job around Bremerton for awhile. It won't be so very long until I'll only have two years to do before quitting. Sometimes I want to quit on 16. What do you sometimes think? Again I think I should train for Pharmacist, because it looks like there will be a long war before I am out and in the dream place.

According to radio reports this country is going to be up against something this Winter. Well, Mr. Kellerman came in. We talked for about two hours about almost everything. He has me believing that the country around Seattle, Washington or Portland, Oregon is good country, if not the best for us to stop in. Well, Babe, do the best you can about money matters and let's hope we will be able to stop for good someplace soon. I am tired of waiting for "tomorrow." Seems that all we have done is to plan on something a year or so in advance and be on the other coast when that year comes around. Pleasant dreams to all.

Wednesday, 29 Dec 1937 on Kanaga Island

This year is very near to a close, isn't it? Have we done very well or very bad this year? I think just so-so. We caught another goose today. That makes us three, now. Will have a whole flock if we keep this up. Think I will try fox trapping one of these days. I should be a pretty good fox trapper, don't you think?

These people are an awful batch of reprobates and thieves. I saw one of the men weighing rice for one of the trappers. He gave him about six pounds of rice and charged him for ten. Union suits sell here for six and eight dollars, shoes for $12 a pair, overalls for $5 a pair. A fellow could get rich in this country. Pleasant dreams to all.

Royse, bearded, in front of the pen where the trapped geese were kept

Thursday, 30 Dec 1937 on Kanaga Island

Babies, all three of you:

Today has been very quiet. No geese this AM. Musick and I fixed a window so it would open this afternoon. Two of the men went hunting. They killed an eagle. The station ship leaves for a trip around the islands tomorrow. They started this morning, but the sea was too rough for them to make landings.

Ellen, I showed your letter to Musick. He thinks you are a very smart girl to write like you do. And Estelle, he wanted to see your toothless grin. He wants to trade his boy for you two girls. I'd never swap you off for any old boy. I love my girls too much. Hope to have a letter from each of you soon, and would love to have a neck hug and lots of kisses, too. Good night. I'll see you in the morning.

Friday, 31 Dec 1937 on Kanaga Island

This year is just about to end. We are about the last of the Americans to see the old year out. This place is right on the 180th meridian, so we could even call yesterday the finish of 1937.

Well, today has been very quiet. Did not catch a goose today. Didn't see any geese in the bay, either. The snow started falling at about 0700, and has been coming down steadily all day. We are having a White New Year. Have made five New Year's Resolutions. Will tell you about them after I see how I make out. Are you turning over any new leaves?

If I just knew how much money we could spare I would get you a pair of fox skins. Do you really want them? Two would cost about $80. The time is almost midnight and I should be asleep. Pleasant dreams to all, and Happy New Year.

Saturday, 1 Jan 1938 on Kanaga Island

Gee Whiz! Another year upon us and the old one just about half gone. Today has been very quiet. Mr. Kellerman caught a goose today. The station ship went out this morning to deliver the trappers to other islands. Tonight after chow Mr. Kellerman and I took the outboard motor in tow and got it to running. He is real proud of the fact that he can make it go. Well, he should be. The motor has been laid up for two months now and we want to go fishing.

This morning I dreamed I was with you. Some way. I was feeling your cheek and you would not do a thing nor say a word. It was a pleasant dream.

About the whiskers again. They are over two months old now and are just like my hair — standing in all directions. This last week has gone by in a hurry. Feb. 1st will soon be here and I can mail this. March will be here shortly after that, and we may pack up and leave here in April. That will be the best time for me. It is now way past midnight, so I'll go to bed and see you in the morning.

Sunday, 2 Jan 1938 on Kanaga Island

Babes:

This morning three of us went fishing. We got five codfish and as usual they were full of worms. After we got back from fishing and put the boat away, I went to the end of the dock and caught four big fish called "Irish lords." They look like heck, and the bay is full of them. So I catch them just to be fishing.

Musick and I are all steamed up over seal hunting. The trappers tell me that we may shoot one about 10 miles from here. Perhaps we will try it. Cowell shot a fox this afternoon. He will get $8 for the skin. They are really too pretty to shoot.

After supper tonight I cleaned up and washed clothes. So now I am all clean for another few days. I certainly need a sewing machine or you to patch some of the underwear and dungarees. Again, pleasant dreams.

Monday, 3 Jan 1938 on Kanaga Island

Today Musick and I cleaned up. Went out hunting. We were after an eagle and that is all that we would shoot at, too. Saw plenty of ducks and geese, but did not bother them. Also we did not get any eagles. We walked all around the bay just because we could, as the weather has been fine. The Dorothea (station ship) came in and brought a few fresh fish. They gave us one piece of halibut, which was quite a change from what we have been putting up with.

This morning we picked up a lot of moonstones on the beach. I suppose I have a quart of them here. Some of them look pretty good. Wonder if they will be like the stones from Hilo. The hour is past 11 PM, so once more I will tell you good night.

Tuesday, 4 Jan 1938 on Kanaga Island

Tonight I am tired. I moved about two tons of coal and scrubbed the house through. Musick baked all day. Had lots of snow yesterday and last night. It seems to be thawing some.

The boat from the island of Adak is coming in here with mail. The week it will take for it to make the trip will seem long. Hope I get a letter or two and a Sears catalog. No more to tell you that I know of right now. The wind is whistling past the house tonight, just like Winter. Good night.

Wednesday, 5 Jan 1938 on Kanaga Island

Tonight I want to write to Estelle. Do you remember the time you cut the straps off Ellen's shoes and the time you "Beeped der Horn"? And are you still my little "weedle puss"? Poppy certainly wants to see his little girls. The ship at Dutch Harbor is supposed to be coming here. I do so hope it has a letter from you and Ellen. Are you doing well in school, baby? I am sure you are doing your lessons like a nice girl. Are you helping Grandma?

Today has been very cold and windy. The snow has been blown off the hills. They are barren and look like they have burned. The tundra moss is a dark green moss and makes them appear burned over.

We turned our geese loose. They would not eat and were flying around in the pens and striking their heads and wings on the sides. I am glad we let them go. One of the trappers caught another fox. I wish you and Ellen could see it. The little foxes are very pretty. Baby, there is no more news to tell you. Good night — I'll see you in the morning. I love both of my little girls.

Poppy

Thursday, 6 Jan 1938 on Kanaga Island

Last night was one of our cold nights. Some of the water pipes froze. Today we put another stove up and moved the onions into another room. I have been pretty busy all day. Have read some, sewed some, and cleaned some. Nothing more to tell you, so I'll sleep some. We don't know yet if we will get mail on the Martha. All of us hope so. Pleasant dreams.

Friday, 7 Jan 1938 on Kanaga Island

Today has been a real nice day, but just like the other days we had breakfast, washed the dishes, swept the floor, and went out hunting for anything. Mr. Kellerman killed a duck, shot at a hawk and a crow. Hit them, too, but he was too far away to kill them. All I did was to lug a rifle along. We crossed a lake that was frozen over. The ice was about six inches thick. Just right to skate on. The volcano certainly looked fine this morning. It is covered with snow right to the peak and has just a haze of smoke at the top. Pleasant dreams.

Saturday, 8 Jan 1938 on Kanaga Island

Dear ones:

Today has been a whiz. We have had sleet, snow, thawing, and wind and rain. Sun shone and shadowed nearly all at the same time, too. I did intend to go to the other side of the island today. The snow this morning scared me out of the trip. This afternoon I brought all the traps in.

Mr. Kellerman took my picture last week. You should see it. I am really a whiz. I have almost three months of beard and have gained about 17 pounds. I weigh 181 now. Dreamed about you last night and have been thinking of you all day. Tonight I got the picture of you and me out. You still look good to me. How do I look to you?

We have no information about the ship which is to bring mail in here. My guess is she won't be here at all. Wonder how much money we have in the bank and if we have all the insurance paid up and if you all are doing alright. Wonder if you ever dream and daydream of me. I do of you. So I'll stop and go to sleep and hope to see all of you in my dreams.

Sunday, 9 January 1938 on Kanaga Island

Woke up this AM — the wind and rain was terrific. All the fires were out and about 20 leaks in the roof. Well, such are the things we put up with in the out-of-the-way places. Musick and me developed pictures this morning. Will send you a print or two of them.

We have stayed close in all day. The weather has been so that we just could not get out. Last night we had ice cream for supper. Made it from Klim* and ice off the lake. Sent you a radiogram tonight. Can't say much in it. It will let you know that I still remember you. Good night.

---

*Klim is a brand of powdered milk, at the time owned by Borden.

<u>Monday, 10 Jan 1938 on Kanaga Island</u>

Today has been warm and pleasant. I woke up about 0730. The rain had stopped, but the clouds and wind were still here. After breakfast Musick and me scrubbed the place. Got out a case of milk, looked through our eggs and found two dozen broken eggs in one can. We got them out and cleaned the others up so they would not absorb the odor.

About 1:30 Musick and I went along the beach to see what the storm has brought in. We saw a lot of driftwood and other stuff that washed in. Musick found two glass balls while I found three. I have six now. We saw lots of ducks and geese. Did not kill any of them, though. Most all the snow has melted away. All the lakes have some mush ice on them.

One afternoon Mr. Kellerman and I went out on the ice to sound the depth of the lake. We found about four feet of water and no bottom to the mud. All the valleys here are filled with mud, with a crust of grass on top of them. If the grass is cut through I suppose a person would sink to China, or Hoboken, in the mud. The little streams sometimes run along the surface, then dive into the ground and run underground for a few feet, then out again.

The Martha leaves Dutch Harbor sometime next week with the mail. I do so hope to get a letter from you. The two weeks I'll have to wait for the ship to get here are going to be very, very long. At the same time the month or six weeks you will have to wait to get this will seem so long, too. Pleasant dreams.

Tuesday, 11 Jan 1938 on Kanaga Island

Well, today has been like most of the other days. We got up, cooked up, cleaned up, loafed, had supper, cleaned up, shot the breeze, and to bed. I bathed, washed clothes, and drank coffee until about five minutes ago. We had wind, sleet, rain, sunshine, and shadows today. Oh yes, before I do forget it – an earthquake this morning about 5 AM. I slept through all of it, so why mention it.

The Martha doesn't leave until next week with the mail and it is doubtful if these people here will pick it up for us. We won't know for another week yet. Am writing all this in pencil and hope to type it out before the Dorothea leaves, and I want to wait until mail comes from you before starting the rewriting. So I'll be pretty busy for an hour or so when I start.

The trappers are coming. They tell tales of lying out in the cold and rain for two days without heat and very little food. I'd never put up with that kind of a life for the pay they get.

Well, if we do not get mail this trip it can't be so long until March. Again I'll say pleasant dreams to all of you and love to my babies.

Thursday, 13 Jan 1937 on Kanaga Island

Babes:

I missed writing to you last night. Got to bed late and was tired. Yesterday was about the same as any other day and today has been just about the same as yesterday. Musick & me went on a duck hunt today and had the usual luck — no luck. We have had rain and snow all day. Tonight the moon is shining through the clouds and rain is falling, too. Tonight I washed some clothes, read awhile and here I am, writing to you with nothing to say. Just about one more week and we will have mail, unless something goes wrong. Good night.

Friday, 14 Jan 1938 on Kanaga Island

Again it is the same old stuff. We have had wind, rain, and snow today. I have spent most of the day reading. Had my hair cut this AM. Fixed a fox cage this afternoon and cleaned up the house between times.

Well, last year about this time what were we doing? I'd rather know what we are going to be doing this time next year.

We have had just about a week of storm. The tide has been almost over the dock a time or two. There is lots of wreckage on the beach — and it is high up on the beach, too. No more to tell you. So again, "I'll see you in the morning. Pleasant dreams."

Saturday, 15 Jan 1938 on Kanaga Island

Today has been windy and cold. Have stayed indoors all day. The water pipes on the dock froze up again. We were without water for a while. Have read nearly all day. Worked a few arithmetic problems.

The time is past midnight. I really have nothing to tell you. Sent you a radiogram tonight. You should get it before this letter gets to you. I think we will get mail next week. I do hope so. Two more of the trappers came in today. They tell stories of hardships and very few furs. Pleasant dreams.

Sunday, 16 Jan 1938 on Kanaga Island

Babes:

Today I did the same things as yesterday. Breakfast, swept, and read awhile. About 12 o'clock I put on about half of the clothes that I own and went out into the snowstorm to look for the goats. We expect one of the nannys to have a kid soon. After she comes fresh we are to milk her. I said we, when I'll have the job.

Tonight I put all the clothes on to soak. Will wash in the AM. The storm has about subsided now, so I suppose the Dorothea will go out in a day or so to get the mail. I most certainly hope so. Sent you a radiogram through an amateur station last night. Wonder if you will ever get it. You can reply through the party who delivers it to you.

This afternoon I thought of lots of things to tell you and now I just can't think of a thing. So I may as well quit and go to bed. Good night. I'll see you in the morning.

<u>Monday, 17 Jan 1938 on Kanaga Island</u>

Dear Babes:

Today has been quiet. The wind was not half as bad today as it has been. Some snow, but not long at a time. We carried coal up to the house this morning – 1000 lbs of it. Musick and me scrubbed the house through this AM. That took most of the morning. I washed a few pieces of clothing out and read the rest of the day. Last night I dreamed of all of you. It was a real pleasant dream, but right now I cannot remember a bit of it.

This is the week that the Martha is to bring the mail in to Adak Island. We have to send over after it. Pleasant dreams.

Tuesday, 18 Jan 1938 on Kanaga Island

On this day Royse Rainey Gibson and his friend Clyde Musick checked out rifles and went to hunt for seals. They never returned, and extensive searches by the Navy never found any sign of the two men.

S. D. MAN LOST IN ALEUTIANS

Navy Hunts Bluejacket, Pal; Fear For Safety

An intensive search was being conducted in the Aleutian Islands today for a San Diego bluejacket, missing since last Wednesday when he left on a hunting expedition, the Navy Department reported in Washington today.

Royce Rayney Gibson, chief pharmacist's mate, of San Diego, was accompanied by Clyde Musick Cook of Burkburnett, Tex., on the trip. Fears were felt for their safety when they were many hours overdue at their station, the Alaskan Aerological Observation Post at Kanga, Aleutian Islands.

The Navy Department said small boats were searching the coast line.

Clipping from the San Diego Union, *January 22, 1938*

The Aftermath

End of January, 1938. The radiogram came with a terse message:

**CHIEF PHARMACIST'S MATE R. R. GIBSON MISSING.
SEARCH IN PROGRESS.**

It wasn't until his personal effects were sent home, much later, that my mother had any description of Kanaga Island. Until then she only knew that it was "adjacent" to Alaska. The Aleutian Islands hadn't yet been well mapped, so for the layman there was very little information about them.

She also had no way of contacting the island. The Red Cross existed, but it was not an organization that could help in this crisis. Any information came second- and third-hand and was incomplete at best.

Speculation was rampant. The Japanese were aggressing. Maybe he was on an ice floe and was picked up and taken to Japan. Maybe he fell into the current and was swept to another part of the island. Maybe the volcano erupted and he was trapped by lava somewhere. All these possibilities were proffered by people who also knew nothing about the terrain or the weather on Kanaga Island.

We were living with my grandmother on Island Avenue. During the time we were there, On and I contracted whooping cough. The public health nurse came to the house and posted a quarantine sign

82

on the front door. Grandma kept tearing it down, and Mom was very upset because the law required it to be posted. I had no perception that Grandma was mentally unstable, but Mom said later that she was a side worry when the telegram came from the Navy.

It was dark when a reporter came to the house. On and I were peeking from behind Mom while she was talking to him at the door. She was whispering because she didn't want Grandma to get upset. She gave him a picture and it appeared with the story in the paper the next day.

I don't remember that Mom ever told us at the time that he was missing. I marvel at how she got through the next weeks.

CHIEF PETTY OFFICER SOUGHT

Royce Rainey Gibson, chief pharmacist's mate, shown here with his wife, has been reported missing since Wednesday from the Alaskan aerological observation post at Kanaga, Aleutian Islands. This picture was taken in October, soon before Gibson was transferred from San Diego to Kanaga.

S. D. Wife Clings to Hope For Missing Navy Man

Local Chief Petty Officer Fails to Return to Alaska Station; Left on Hunting Trip; Boat Search Begun.

"He's not officially dead yet."

With this slender hope for consolation, Mrs. Royce Rainey Gibson, 2529 Island ave., waited anxiously at her home last night for word concerning her husband who is missing from the Alaskan aerological observation post at Kanaga, Aleutian islands.

Gibson, chief pharmacists' mate, and a companion, Clyde Music, cook, of Bowie, Tex., failed to return from a hunt Wednesday, The Associated Press reported from Washington. A search is being made. The navy department said the observation post is small and the number of men available for the search is limited. A small boat is searching the coast line.

The effects of the report were visible on Mrs. Gibson's face as she waited with the couple's two children, Ellen, 5, and Estelle, 7, in their modest home.

While the trio sat in the front room Mrs. G. R. Steele, Mrs. Gibson's mother, lay ill in another room. She was not told her son-in-law is missing.

Gibson, born in Kelley, Okla., formerly was stationed here aboard the U. S. S. Gamble. He left here last October when he was transferred to Kanaga. Mrs. Gibson learned that her husband was missing Friday in a telegram from the navy department.

Gibson's parents reside in New Mexico.

Article from the San Diego Union, *January 23, 1938*

Royse's parents were living in Elida, New Mexico. Their rural household had no electricity, no telephone, and no access to the wider world. Several days after the news of their son's disappearance was broadcast on radio, a distant relative from Burkburnett, Texas, contacted someone in Elida who relayed the news of Royse's disappearance.

Later someone provided a newspaper article stating that Clyde Musick from a local Burkburnett family and another man, Royse Gibson from San Diego, "went missing" while on Naval duty in the Aleutian Islands.

Other newspaper articles followed, in San Diego and New Mexico. And Royse's brother and father sought help from Senator Carl Hatch to find out more.

FORMER CITIZEN LOST IN ALASKA SINCE JAN. 19

Miss Nellie Gibson received word Sunday that her nephew, Rainey Gibson, is lost in the Alaska wastes.

Mr. Gibson and another member of an Alaskan aerological observation crew at Kanaya, Aleutian Islands, failed to return from a hunt Wednesday, January 19, and are still missing, although an intensive search is being made for them.

Rainey is a chief pharmacist's mate and his wife and children live in San Diego, California. He attended school at Gould several years ago and he and his family have visited here on several occasions. He will have spent 20 years in the Navy next May at which time he will be entitled to retire on a pension.

Hope is still held for his safety and relatives are expecting favorable reports any time.

An article, probably from the Albuquerque Democrat, *published on January 24, 1938*

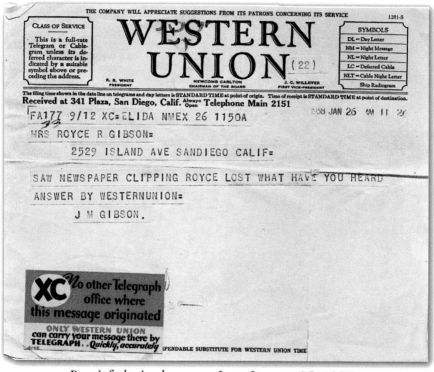

Royse's father's telegram to Ione, January 25, 1937

Former Gould Man Disappears In Alaska While Seal Hunting

The Democrat is in receipt of a detailed account of the disappearance of Rainey Gibson and companion on January 18 in Alaska as submitted to us by Mr. Gibson's aunt, Miss Nellie Gibson of Gould. The details were sent her by Ross R. Kellerman, Lieutenant, U. S. Navy, in whose company Chief Gibson was listed at the time of his disappearance. Summary of events regarding the account and hunt that followed are briefly given herewith:

"At 094 5 Gibson requested permission to go seal hunting, C. Musick to accompany him. Gibson stated that they were going to hunt for seal in the vicinity of an inlet known as 'Haystack' and then were going to dig in an abandoned native village. At 1045 they left the station carrying with them two service one shovel, one flashlight, and some things in gunnysacks slung on their backs. The ground was covered with about three inches of snow and the wind force was variable due to passing light snow squalls. At 1600 the men did not return to the station. At 1920 Lt. Kellerman and GRM Conyngham left the station to head in the general direction of Haystack, and at 2000 yards from camp the trail of the two men was found and believed to be that of Gibson and Musick. This trail was followed about two miles when it became so indistinct in the darkness that it could no longer be followed. At 1920 Mr. Clark and a native left camp to hunt the beach trail to Adak Strait. At 2200 both searching parties returned. At 2240 Caerog Cowell and RM3C Rodman set out for Haystack cabin and returning at 0400, being unable to locate the cabin due to darkness and difficulty in traveling. At 0810 Kellerman, Erwin and a native left for Haystack cabin and arrived there at 1000 but found no evidence of anyone having been there in some time. At 1005 the native was directed to return to Kanaga Bay and re-

port facts to Mr. Clark, manager of the Kanaa Ranching Company. The rest of the party returned by way of the beach. At 1240 Mr. Clark departed in the company boat Dorothea to search the beach Adak Strait. At 1510 the searching party returned and at 1630 Dorothea returned.

"A general conference of all men on the island was held at 1700 to determine the best method of general search of the entire island. On January 20 at 0700 Dorothea departed Kanaga Bay and at 0800 three searching parties left the station to search lakes and island. On January 21 at 0700 the crew of the Dorothea left the station again and two more Navy personnel departed for the search. At 1600 three searching parties returned to the station. On January 23 three searching parties remaining out returned. In all this hunt not a single trace of either men was found.

"On January 24 and 25 several parties searched in the vicinity of Kanaga Bay and the beach of Adak Strait. On January 25 the search was abandoned except that occasional patrols of the beach in the vicinity of Kanaga Bay were to be continued in case bodies were washed up on the beach."

The final decision of Lieutenant Kellerman was that "It is believed beyond a question of doubt that the disappearance of Gibson, R. R. and Musick, C., was due to the death of both men and that their death was in the line of duty."

An article from the Albuquerque Democrat, probably from late January, 1938

11 February 1938

Subject: GIBSON, Royse Rainey
         Chief Pharmacist's Mate, U.S.Navy.

My dear Mr. Gibson:

This Bureau desires to acknowledge receipt of your telegram of 8 February 1938, requesting the details incident to the disappearance of Royse Rainey Gibson, Chief Pharmacist's Mate, U.S. Navy.

In replying, you are advised that at present the official report of the investigation conducted in connection with the disappearance of Royse Rainey Gibson, and his companion, Clyde Musick, Ship's Cook first class, U.S.Navy, has not been received, and the reports received from the Officer in Charge of the Alaskan Aerological Expedition, at Kanaga Island, Alaska, have been made by despatch, and are somewhat fragmentary.

It appears that GIBSON, and his companion, MUSICK, left the Expedition Headquarters on a hunting trip, and were due to return on January 19th, 1938. Upon failing to return, searching parties were organized and sent out immediately, and on the early morning of January 20th, additional native parties were employed in the search. Boats circled the island, and search of the beaches and cabins were made, but unfortunately, no trace of the men could be found, and their fate remains undetermined.

The Officer in Charge of the Expedition has repeatedly mentioned that the extreme weather conditions greatly retarded the progress of their search, but in view of the nature of the terrain, it was his own opinion that both men were drowned either by falling through the ice in one of the many lakes, or by falling from a cliff into the ocean.

However, as stated, the complete report of the search has not been received, and the Bureau is now without the facts upon which the Officer in Charge of the Expedition based his opinion.

Pending the receipt of the report of the investigation and search, and its approval by the Secretary of the Navy, these men can only be carried as "missing", and no action can be taken by the Navy Department towards the settlement of their affairs, and the payment of death benefits to their dependents.

Sincerely yours,

Adolphus Andrews,
Chief of Bureau.

C. B. Hatch,
By direction.

A February 11, 1938 letter in response to a February 8 telegram from Royse's brother, Pat Gibson of Belen, New Mexico, inquiring about payment of a death benefit for Ione and her daughters

87

A telegram appealing for help, sent by Royse's parents in Elida, New Mexico, on February 24, 1938, to Senator Carl Hatch

NAVY WILL SEARCH FOR LOST NEW MEXICO MAN

WASHINGTON, Feb. 25 (AP)— Sen. Carl Hatch pressed today for a renewed search for two Navy men, one of them a New Mexican, who disappeared Jan. 19 while hunting on Kanaga Island in the Aleutians.

Royce Rainey Gibson, son of Mrs. J. N. Gibson of Elida, N. M., and Clyde Musick are the missing men. Sen. Hatch said the Navy Department had promised a thorough search for them when weather permitted.

Mrs. Gibson had appealed to the senator for aid in finding her son.

A February 25 newspaper article (left), probably from the Albuquerque Democrat, indicates that Senator Hatch had taken action.

Meanwhile, for my mother the only access to information was through radiogram contact — frustrating and expensive. Royse disappeared in January, but my mother never received any official information other than the initial radiogram until she wrote on April 3rd to the District Commander in Seattle. His response appears on pages 90–92. This letter gave her the first formal information about what the fate of her husband might be.

8 April 1938

Mrs. Royse R. Gibson
Box 238
Julian, Calif.

My Dear Mrs. Gibson,

I have your letter dated 3 April 1938 in connection
with the disappearance of your husband, Royse Rainey
Gibson, Chief Pharmacist Mate, USN.
You are aware that your husband was reported missing
since Jan. 19th, 1938, when, with his companion, he failed
to return to his station. Mr. G and his companion had
gone on a hunting trip and when they failed to return at
appointed time the officer in charge ordered a search.
At this time weather conditions were mild. It was fairly
cold, some snow, and the lakes were covered with ice.
The personnel at the station searched all night for the
missing men.
Two searchers followed their trail for a considerable
distance, but lost it on a stretch of bare ground, from
which the snow had evidently been blowing. This is the
last evidence found of either man.
The day following that on which the men disappeared
a general search was conducted by Naval personnel
assisted by the island's native inhabitants and later
by Coast Guard. The Coast Guard made a thorough search
of the beach surrounding the island, while searching
parties ashore divided into groups of two men each were
assigned sections to be searched. No trace found. This
method of search was halted the third day by a severe
storm which lasted a week. When weather conditions again
permitted the search was continued for several weeks, the
entire island being covered by searching parties, without
success.
The island in question contains approximately 75
square miles and has many inland lakes. The terrain is
cut up considerably by gorges and numerous small lakes,
and in places along the coastline sheer cliffs arise from
the surrounding waters of the seas. It is believed by
searchers that (the men) may have fallen through the ice
of a lake or into a deep snow-filled gorge, from which
they were unable to extricate themselves.
The storm which halted the searchers in all
probability obliterated any evidence which might have

led to the finding of the missing men. There remains the possibility that the men may have fallen over a cliff into the ocean, but this is not believed to be the case.

In February the USS Swallow was dispatched to the island to bring in stores and replacements for the two missing men and to conduct a board of investigation into the circumstances surrounding the disappearance of the missing men. Although the Swallow (minesweeper) stayed off the coast of the island, the personnel reached shore and investigation was conducted.

The report of this investigation has now reached the Navy Department. Although there appears to be no question of doubt in the minds of those cognizant of the facts surrounding the case that the two men are dead, it is necessary that the Navy Dept make every effort to locate the bodies of the men before declaring them dead.

It is believed quite possible that the bodies will be found when the snow and ice have melted on the island. This should be sometime in the late Spring or early Summer, and as soon as weather conditions are favorable another search is to be conducted.

Until the Navy Dept declares your husband dead, the Commandant is not in a position to take any action towards the disposal of your husband's effects, or to otherwise act under the assumption that your husband is dead. The circumstances surrounding are such that, in my opinion, the matter should be definitely settled by Fall of this year.

I deeply regret that the course which the Navy Dept is compelled to take is causing you such inconvenience, and wish to assure you that the case will be cleared at the earliest possible date. I shall keep you advised of any information which may come to hand bearing upon the case.

Very sincerely,
W. J. Giles*

---

*W. J. Giles signed the last two entries in Royse Gibson's duty book, showing him to be Gibson's Commanding Officer at the 13th Naval District in Seattle, Washington. Gibson's daughter Estelle Gibson Lauer typed this transcription of his letter many years later from the original handwritten document, which is shown on page 92.

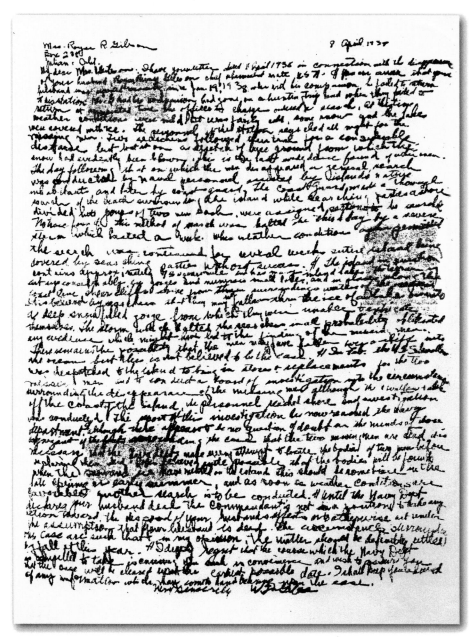

W. J. Giles sent a handwritten letter to Ione Gibson on April 8, 1938, in response to her radiogram of April 3 seeking information about her husband's disappearance.

When Lt. Kellerman on Kanaga Island had determined to his satisfaction that Gibson and Musick would not be found alive, he contacted the naval base in Seattle and requested that a marker recognizing the disappearance of the two men be delivered to Kanaga. The men who had replaced the original party put the monument on a sledge and hauled it to the hillside above the base.

According to the letter from Commander Giles (on pages 90–91), Royse's effects couldn't be returned to his family until the fall, after a summer search of the island had been completed. However, by that time the aerological expedition had been evacuated from Kanaga, and Lieutenant Kellerman had already gathered the belongings of the two men and sent them to their next of kin.

IN MEMORY OF
R. R. GIBSON, C. PH. M. U.S.N.
C. MUSICK, S. C. 1C. U.S.N.

MEMBERS OF THE UNITED
STATES NAVY ALASKAN
AEROLOGICAL EXPEDITION
WHO LOST THEIR LIVES
IN LINE OF DUTY ON
JANUARY 18, 1938

ERECTED BY
MEMBERS OF THE PARTY

Kellerman sent the families of Gibson and Musick photos of the monument and copies of the blueprint.

Uncertainty

Money was a looming problem. While Royse was stationed on Kanaga, my mother received an allotment for herself and for On and me. While we were living with Grandma, housing was not an expense. But Grandma wasn't stable, and the crisis made it hard to keep things on an even keel. Legalities dictated that, in instances where there was no body, a year must pass before a declaration of death could be issued. Mom had no job skills and certainly had no prospects of earning enough money to pay for housing. At least a year stretched ahead before she could collect life insurance and a pension that would enable her to provide a house for the three of us.

She had always held the Masonic Lodge in high regard. Royse had proudly joined the Order when they lived in Vallejo, before being stationed in Hawaii. The creed dictated that the Brotherhood would take care of widows and orphans. So she contacted the Naval Lodge in Vallejo to request forms to enable her to send On and me to the Masonic Home in Covena until she could find a way for us to be together again.

The thought is chilling. I know she was acting in the face of panic. A friend who had grown up in an orphanage intervened, and Mom sought another solution.

ERNEST CHARLES FUGLER, *Master*
428 El Dorado Street
Telephone 1129-J

BERT CORY WHITELEY, *Secretary*
Post Office Box 87
Telephone 1306

NAVAL LODGE No. 87

F. & A. M.

Stated Meetings First Thursday of Each Month

Vallejo, California,

Aug. 6, 1938.

Mrs. Royse R. Gibson,
3578 Polk St.,
San Diego,
California

Dear Mrs. Gibson:-

       We have your letter of July 6th.in which you enclose a copy of a letter received from the Acting Judge Advocate of the Navy. The letter is practically the same as the one we received. I understand that the case will be reviewed soon after Jan. 18, 1939.

       I am sending an application blank that must be filled out before a child can be entered into the Masonic Home at Covena, near Los Angeles. By reading it carefully, you will understand what is necessary. If you wish to send your daughters there, I will send you another blank so that you will have one for each daughter. We are so far away that it is impossible to help you with your problems. I am sure that R.P. Wakeman, Secretary of the Masonic Board of Relief in San Diego, Masonic Temple, San Diego, will be willing to assist you in our behalf.

       Trusting this will find you and the children well, I remain

       Very truly yours,

B. C. Whiteley
Secretary.

A letter from Naval Lodge No. 87 (Vallejo) in answer to Ione's request for help of July 6, 1938

We moved to Julian, in the mountains near San Diego, and lived with Mom's brother and his wife and baby for the next few months. There was no kindergarten for me, but On finished second grade there. Every morning a truck came from Banner with a flock of milk goats that were set to graze on some hillside in Julian. On, the extra passenger, joined the goats and was dropped off at school. She complained bitterly and she did take on a bit of their odor.

By the time school was out, Mom had made arrangements for us to move back to San Diego, where she had found housing and a job. We would live with Dorothy Witcher and Sam, her father. Dorothy had developed crippling arthritis when she was young and needed someone to help take care of her.

On and I attended third and first grades at Logan Elementary while we lived with Dorothy and Sam on Newton Avenue. I didn't find the situation odd. During the Depression it seemed to be the norm for households to expand and contract. Periodically other people lived there and slept wherever there was a spot. Martha Rae stayed for awhile. Her brother Bill was a baker who worked the night shift and slept on the couch in the daytime. Their sister Jean also put in appearances. During school vacations, Dorothy's two daughters stayed too. The house had two small bedrooms and a screened-in porch where Sam slept.

I assume that Mom was getting the dependents' allotment until the year was up and Royse could be declared dead. After that she could collect a pension for herself and allotments for On and me until we reached 18.

The Determination of Death was reported in a declaration from the Judge Advocate General of the Navy, which was approved by the Acting Secretary of the Navy on February 3, 1939. The report (transcribed) is shown on pages 97–100.

DEPARTMENT OF THE NAVY
OFFICE OF THE JUDGE ADVOCATE GENERAL
WASHINGTON, D.C.

From: The Judge Advocate General.
To: The Secretary of the Navy.

Subject: Royse Rainey Gibson, chief pharmacist's mate,
             and Clyde Musick, ship's cook first class,
             U. S. Navy - Determination of death.

References: (a) Investigation convened to inquire into
             disappearance of subject-named men.
             (b) J.A.G. let. of Jan. 13, 1939, file
             MM-Gibson, R.R./A17-26 (380308).
             (c) Bu. M.& S. 1st Ind. of Jan. 19, 1939,
             file P3-666681 1068912o
             (d) BuNav. 2nd Ind. of Jan. 24, 1939, file
             Nav64-EVH.

1. Under date of February 21, 1938, an investigation
was convened at the Alaska Aerological Expedition, Kanaga
Island, Alaska, for the purpose of inquiring into the circumstances surrounding the disappearance of Royse Rainey
Gibson, chief pharmacist's mate, and Clyde Musick, ship's cook
first class, U. S. Navy, which occurred on January 18,
1938.

2. The evidence offered before the investigation
did not establish the cause of the disappearance of Gibson
and Musick. However, the investigating officer expressed
the opinion that the two men died on January 18, 1938,
apparently as the result of being washed off a reef. In
acting upon the record of proceedings of the investigation,
the Secretary of the Navy directed that the above-named
men be carried on the rolls of the Bureau of Navigation as
missing for a period of one year from January 18, 1938, and
that upon the expiration of that period the case again be
referred to the Judge Advocate General for further consideration. In accordance with these instructions this case is
now before this office for consideration as to whether or
not Gibson and Musick may be held to be deceased.

3. The evidence offered before the above-mentioned investigation shows that on January 18, 1938, at about 11:00 a.m., Gibson and Musick left the headquarters of the Alaskan Aerological Expedition, Kanaga Island, for the purpose of proceeding upon a seal-hunting expedition at a place in the vicinity of a cabin known as "Haystack Cabin", located on Adak Strait, to the northeast and about four miles from the station. They were scheduled to return at about 4:00 p.m. On the trip they wore wind and rain-proof outer clothing and shoe packs, and carried two service rifles, one shovel, a flashlight and other miscellaneous equipment.

4. When Gibson and Musick failed to return to the station, the Commanding Officer organized a searching party and at about 7:20 p.m., on January 18, this party proceeded along the trail which the men were assumed to have followed. A trail made by two men going in the direction intended to be followed by Gibson and Musick was picked up in the snow, which led to a lake where it turned and skirted the shore to the opposite side. About one-half mile beyond the lake the trail was lost due to drifting snow. Further search and display of flashlights from a high knoll failed to reveal any evidence of the missing men.

5. At 8:00 a.m., on January 19, a party consisting of the Commanding Officer of the Expedition, a native guide and an enlisted man proceeded to "Haystack Cabin." It was immediately evident that no one had recently been in or around the cabin. A search of the beaches along Adak Strait was then undertaken in the "DOROTHEA", a boat owned by the Kanaga Ranching Company, which covered the entire shore line of Kanaga Island bordering on Adak Strait, but with no results. Parties were then organized to make a complete search of the Island with the "DOROTHEA" completely circling the Island and searching all beaches from the water side. This search lasted for three days, but without result.

6. Subsequently, searches were made by naval personnel and trappers on the Island and on May 31, 1938, an airplane attached to the U. S. Coast Guard Cutter SPENCER flew over the Island observing the bottoms of lakes and the coast line around the circumference of the Island, but no evidence of the missing men was discovered.

98

7. The officer in charge of the Aerological Expedition, Lieutenant R. R. Kellerman, U. S. Navy, testified before the investigation that he did not believe that it would have been possible for Gibson and Musick to have left the Island alive since all known small boats had been accounted for and the Expedition had observed no vessels of any type in the vicinity of Kanaga Island since arrival except naval vessels and the "DOROTHEA".

8. It appears from the evidence that it would have been possible for the men to have lived on the Island for a limited time using birds as food, but that in order to have done so the men would have had to resort to the use of their guns, and no shots were heard by searching parties other than those fired by members of these parties. Likewise no fires were observed at any time. There is no indication that either of the men desired to desert the naval service, or would otherwise have remained absent from their station except for the occurrence of an accident preventing their return.

9. It is a well-established rule of law that mere unexplained absence is not sufficient to warrant a determination of death unless it is continued for a period of seven years. (Davie vs. Briggs, 97 U.S. 628; Salmon Bay Sand and Gravel Company vs. Marshall, 93 Fed. (2d) 1; C.M.O. 2, 1935, 23; C.M.O. 3, 1937, 4) However, in cases where the evidence establishes exposure of a missing person to some specific impending or immediate peril or danger which might reasonably destroy life, or where the circumstances in any case are inconsistent with the continuance of life, it is not necessary to resort to the presumption of death after sevan years' unexplained absence, and prior to that time death may legally be held to have occurred. (Davie vs. Briggs, 97 U.S. 628; Fidelity Mutual Life Association vs. Mettler, 185 U.S. 308; U.S. vs. Hayman et al., 62 Fed. (2d) 118; Salmon Bay Sand and Gravel Company vs. Marshall, 93 Fed. (2d) 1; Penn Mutual Life Insurance Company vs. Tilton, 84 Fed. (2d) 10; Mutual Life Insurance Company of New York vs. Zimmerman et al., 75 Fed. (2d), 758; C.M.O. 2, 1935, 23)

10. Upon a consideration of the evidence available in this case it would appear that the sealing trip which Gibson and Musick had undertaken on Kanaga Island was a

hazardous enterprise that took place in the middle of
winter on a sparsely-inhabited island on which there was
considerable snow and ice which might easily have caused
these men to slip into the water or through a hole in the
ice into a lake or the sea and be lost without evidence
remaining as to what had occurred. Kanaga Island is one
of the Aleutian group off the coast of Alaska, is sparsely
inhabited and the search made for the two men eliminated
almost to a certainty any conclusion that they might have
been alive on the Island for any substantial period of time
after January 18, 1938.

11. There was no evidence that the two men had any
intention of leaving the island or were dissatisfied with
the naval service and desired to desert. If such had been
the case they would hardly have selected an isolated place
such as Kanaga Island from which to desert. Any presumption of intent to desert is likewise overcome by the fact
that Gibson was a chief petty officer and Musick a petty
officer first class, and both men had considerable naval
service, Gibson having had approximately twenty years'
service and Musick more than thirteen years' service.
Furthermore all known boats on the island were accounted
for, none of which could have been used by the two men to
leave the island.

12. It is the opinion of this office that the evidence
discussed above indicates the existence of facts that are
inconsistent with the continuance of life in the cases of
the above-named men and that they may legally be declared
to be dead. It is the further opinion of this office that
the evidence warrants a determination that their deaths
occurred on January 18, 1938, on which date they proceeded
on the sealing expedition from which they failed to return,
and that their deaths were not the result of their own
misconduct.

W. B. WOODSON.
Acting Secretary of the Navy.

Moving On

Royse had bought a Prudential Double Indemnity Life Insurance policy before he left for the Aleutians. Because no body was recovered, the company would not pay double. Mom went to a lawyer and was told that because she was a woman there was no point in pursuing the claim. She argued, to no avail, that the Navy had declared him dead without recovering a body. She settled for the single life insurance payment of $5,000. With part of it she bought our cabin in Julian, which had to be outfitted with electricity and plumbing. We moved to Julian in the summer of 1939.

Even though logic told her that her husband was dead, we always spoke of him as "lost" or "disappeared." Without a definite ending there was always a possibility that he would be found and come back to us. When Japan surrendered she watched the newspapers for names of released prisoners. She even speculated that he might be in a Siberian prison camp. She never really accepted his death.

And she kept him alive to On and me. She quoted his humor — some of it was earthy: "Not a creature was stirring, not even a mouse stirred" — he ran the words together so the line sounded like "not even a mouse turd."

She often said, "Your Daddy would have enjoyed that," or "Your Daddy used to say...." We knew stories of his childhood and stories of his Navy adventures. We knew where they had traveled and who their friends were. She described his habits and his likes and dislikes.

He was very orderly. I have his notebook with lists of things to be done; the accomplishments were crossed out. My Uncle Pat Gibson told me that once when "Rainey" came to visit he showed them how he had packed his "kit." (His family always called him Rainey, but Mom always called him by his first name.) The toothpaste tube was rolled tightly and put in its place. His towel and washcloth and soap dish were in their appointed places. There was not a millimeter of space for extras. (I have noted many times that I have married my father!)

Mom never let us forget that we had a father to be proud of. It's kind of interesting that, as I got older, I outgrew referring to him as my Daddy. References became more formal. A "Daddy" becomes "Dad" or "Pop." But because we didn't evolve to that stage together, it didn't feel right. "My Father" is not personal. So I grew to calling him Royse.

Mom kept in close touch with my grandparents in New Mexico. I can remember writing to them because Mom "made us." (We had to write the rough draft on a paper bag, and after she had edited it we wrote on real paper.) She also sent my grandmother $1.00 inside a card every Christmas. After a while she realized that Grandma was buying seed with it, so she started sending her dresses (usually from Sears Roebuck). Mom sewed our clothes and she always sent the scraps for Grandma to make quilts from. When Ron and I got married, Grandma sent us a quilt with some of those scraps in it. (Years later she made quilts and sold them to tourists.)

There wasn't much social life in Julian. Mom was in the Women's Club, and aside from meeting in each others' homes and sending the kids out while they told questionable jokes, I don't know what their activities were. She joined the Eastern Star and went to Ramona one night a month for the meetings. The school was the center for gatherings. Anytime there was a program people came out of the woodwork to attend.

We were happy there. As far as I knew there was never any turmoil.

One time Mom got very sick — bronchitis, maybe pneumonia. I missed the security of having her available for our routine. Stella Lane, one of the neighbors, told us that we had to come to her house for dinner every night. She fed us broccoli — which was foreign to me, but I sensed that emergency behavior was required, so I ate it without protest.

When Mom wanted to move into the faster lane, we'd come down to San Diego for the weekend. She'd leave us with Grandma, and she and Esther, her friend, would go dancing at the Trianon Ballroom.

A Marine named Wayne came to Julian to visit us. We all went on a picnic to Borrego. He wanted to marry her but he was five or six years younger. On was approaching her teens and Mom knew this wasn't a good combination.

Herman Beumann, a farmer from Olivenhain, came to visit once. His sister was Mom's high school friend. Mom invited him for dinner and we had a tablecloth and candles. On and I giggled and made improper comments. Herman never came back. For years we teased her about her boyfriend, Herman. Mom would say, "Don't laugh. If I hadn't met your Daddy, Herman might have been your father." That image shut us up.

With the advent of war came inflation. The pension check just wasn't making it. I was nine and On was eleven. Mom got a job as a waitress at the Julian Hotel. She thought she could work out a schedule so she could be home with us. But I can remember coming home from school to a cold empty house. On either took it upon herself or was instructed to take charge. "You have to mind me because I'm the eldest." (I suspect she picked that word up at Sunday School). I bought into that as long as I could, and then I rebelled. "Yeah! Well, you'll die first." I don't remember how long Mom worked at the hotel. She used to bring home her tips in change and we'd sit at the table and count the money.

In the summer of 1941, I played with Harry, Junior and Dick Casey, whose family came up from the desert town of Brawley every summer. Kids are magnets, and we discovered each other. Their Uncle Ward would sometimes come up on weekends to escape the heat. I don't know how they got together but he and Mom visited back and forth. During the winter he came courting. One time we came home from school and he was at our house. They were drinking tea. Later Mom was embarrassed to find that the milk she had served with tea had gone sour. She said to Margaret Casey, Ward's sister-in-law, "I hope Ward didn't get sick from the bad milk." Margaret's response was, "Don't worry about him. He has a cast iron stomach."

Ward came up to Julian often that winter. Sometimes we would go fishing at Lake Henshaw, and since he had a pickup I got to ride in the back with the wind whistling past my ears. I thought this was heaven. He took On and me to the drugstore and bought us ice cream cones. He bought me a pack of Black Jack gum that I rationed out, one per day. I stashed the ABC (already-been-chewed) gum on the board over my bottom bunk when I went to sleep. I finally realized it had run its course when it made me sick to re-re-rechew it.

It was not a love match. My mother and Ward each needed a partner, for different reasons. Ward was 45 years old and realized that the opportunity was past for making his own family, and here was a nice widow with two nice children. Mom knew that the financial stability of our home was a bit shaky. I also think she was weary of the struggle of making ends meet. She expected a new marriage to put her back into the mainstream of life.

One day we went on a picnic to Borrego. Ward suggested that On and I "go for a walk to the top of those rocks." When we looked back, Mom was leaning against a rock and he was facing her with both hands against the rock. They were talking, and On and I were anxiously observing, "I bet he's going to kiss her."

That evening after Ward had left, Mama was lying on the couch. She said, "Come here. I want to talk to you both." Then she told us that Ward had asked her to marry him. On said, "What would Daddy think?" Mama said, "Daddy would want us to be happy."

They were married in June and we moved to Brawley in September. Our lives took on two levels. The second level was to fill in the empty spots of her new marriage with memories of Royse. On and I learned that we shouldn't talk about him in front of Ward. On started calling Ward "Daddy." I couldn't do that so I called him "Pop." Later, in fun, I called him "Wardo." Our Gibson history went underground, and when Pop wasn't around Mom often talked about "your Daddy."

* * *

Mom died in 1964, when she was fifty-nine. Royse had died when she was thirty-two. They had been married for just eight years but the union lasted all her life.

Back to Kanaga

It was after Pop died in 1987 that my husband, Ron, and I began to inquire about access to Kanaga. To have done so earlier would have seemed somehow hurtful to this man who had taken good care of my mother, my sister and me.

We had pictures of the buildings Royse had described in his diary. We had the images of the many lakes and the tundra he spent so much time exploring. We wondered about the digs that had occupied so much of his time. And we especially wanted to see the monument to the two men that sits on a windblown hill overlooking the bay.

Among Royse's effects was a photo of the aerological expedition's base on Kanaga Bay.

We thought we could fly to Adak, the adjacent island, and somehow get from there to our destination. But when we inquired, Naval Air Facility Adak wouldn't give us the time of day. It was a military base and only military personnel and their dependents were allowed on the island. We contacted the school district there to see if some teacher would sponsor us, but we got no answer. We wrote, offering our labor, to an archeology professor from Indiana who was planning a dig on Kanaga. He ignored us.

It really wasn't feasible to try in earnest until the summer of 1995, when we were finally free to go and solvent enough to afford it. The cold war had ended, so we tried Adak again. It was still hopeless, so we contacted Peninsula Airways (PenAir). We would fly to Anchorage on Alaska Airlines and from there on PenAir to the settlement of Unalaska. We could charter a Grumman Goose prop-jet amphibian and pilot for $1,000 per hour of flying time plus $100 an hour "down time." The flight from Unalaska to Kanaga would take about three hours each way. We established that the best weather time would be late July or early August. Our instructions were to "dress warmly."

We sent for every map of Kanaga that was in print. We found Memorial Point and on some maps "Memorial Bay." We reread Royse's diary to sift out all the details of terrain. We knew the layout by heart.

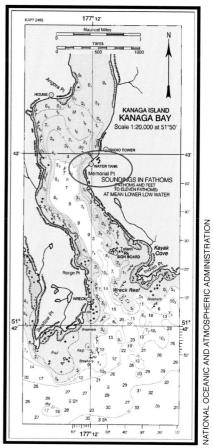

We found Memorial Point on the eastern shore of Kanaga Bay.

Our flight to Anchorage was in the usual big plane — three and two across with flight attendants taking orders for food and drinks. Our flight from Anchorage to Unalaska was in a turbo-prop Metroliner. There were 18 passengers — nine on each side, so there was no fighting over window seats. It took forever to get the baggage loaded because the weight had to be distributed. Our stuff kept being rotated from the nose to the back. Finally the stairs unfolded from the hull and we clambered on board. Ron and I chose the very back seats so the wings wouldn't block our view.

When 18 people were cinched in, the first officer came into the cabin and announced, "Look under your seat. If you have the box of nuts and crackers, you're traveling First Class. If you drank too much coffee, the unisex toilet is in the compartment behind the last seat. There are ear plugs in the pocket in front of you. If you have any questions, feel free to ask us."

It was too noisy to talk but not so noisy that we needed the ear plugs. When we were into the flight, I checked out the toilet. It was a port-a-potty and one could only sit and then crawl back to the cabin. There was a "no smoking" sign, but even if I had had a nicotine fit, the toilet's surroundings weren't conducive to lingering. The wind was whistling through the compartment and I could look through a crack at my suitcase in the baggage bin.

The turbo-prop Metroliner, ready for the trip from Anchorage to Unalaska

We were flying high enough to be over the clouds that obscured the scenery. The two men who were sitting in front of us yelled answers when we asked questions, but we couldn't carry on much conversation. (One was a fisherman who would leave for the Bering Sea the next day. The other was a Dane who had some kind of scientific equipment to try out.)

When we landed in the town of Unalaska, we contacted Mark Greig, who would be our pilot to Kanaga. He told us that the weather was so "iffy" that we'd have to check with him every morning to find out if "today could be the day."

We had arranged to stay at The Bunkhouse, a room-and-board facility where mostly fishermen stayed. It was surprisingly cheap for an isolated spot — $50 a night for both of us, plus $7.50 apiece for dinner and $4 for a sack lunch. Our pilot had told us to leave a "window" of several days to pick the best weather day for flying, so we reserved our Bunkhouse room for six days.

We moved in. On the ensuing two "not today" weather reports, we took the opportunity to explore this frontier town.

We learned that during the winter the unifying organization was the school system. A very modern gym housed equipment for almost every sport. Athletic competitions were the focus for socializing. And in the Spring the Senior class had to top off its finale with a prom. Our hostel hostess described that event. Radio contact with communities on the other islands matched up "dates," and bush pilots provided transportation to unite the couples. Because this would be a memorable event in their children's lives, mothers got together to create prom dresses. We didn't find out whether tuxedos were available or if suits were sufficient to dress up the boys. Everyone who could move came to the prom. In its modernity, instead of local musicians whose offerings might have been questionable, someone served as a disc jockey.

We spent time walking through the community. We visited the graveyard and noted the slanted crossbars that identified Russian Christian crosses. Also there were multi-graves of people who had died in the worldwide flu epidemic of 1918. We learned later that worldwide more people died of that plague than were killed in the World War.

There was a "museum" in a storefront that displayed a translated "diary" written by a Japanese doctor. The last entries were in the form of a letter to his wife and two children. In 1943 when American troops landed on Attu to drive the invaders out, someone retrieved this record of the battle.

The doctor was saying good-bye. The translation didn't identify the gender of either child, but one was four years old and the other was four months. It was a very tender declaration of his love for them.

Additional descriptions told of the invasion by Americans. The island of Kiska had already been reclaimed, and it was obvious that Attu also would return to American hands. The doctor detailed that, by radio, the Japanese soldiers had been given permission from the Emperor to commit suicide. The doctor's responsibility was to provide the means to accomplish such acts. He explained how he had distributed his store of morphine. And now the officers were allotting hand grenades.

* * *

Mark had suggested that since our landing in Kanaga Bay was iffy — he didn't know how close we could get to the shore in the bay — we might want to get some hip- or waist-high waders. We naively asked where we could rent some. He was tactful and suggested that we go to Carl's, the local department store.

We found out that no one rented waders. They're vital equipment for a fisherman's livelihood and they cost about $100. Since we'd have limited use for them after our adventure, we sought another solution.

Although poorly compartmentalized, Carl's would have been competition for Walmart. Wedding rings were next to fishing poles and down jackets. Greeting cards intermingled with milk of magnesia. Flannel pajamas shared shelf space with metal buckets.

On a shelf over cans of kerosene was the solution to our landing dilemma. It was a raft priced at $50, proclaiming space for two persons. At the counter we were assured we could return our purchase if we didn't need it and the box was unopened. Later, upon landing in the bay at our destination, we would discover that the raft was gaily decorated with Mickey Mouse and Donald Duck, and that it was designed for two *small* passengers.

* * *

Every morning Mark called with a weather report. After two "not todays," on Wednesday he said, "Today and tomorrow look good."

I said, "Let's go today."

Ron and I got to the airport in plenty of time — Mark was still checking out the plane. There would be enough fuel in the tanks to get us to Kanaga, but to get us back to Unalaska he'd have to hand-pump fuel from barrels inside the plane into the wing tanks.

We had to distribute our weight to balance the barrels of fuel. Coming back it wouldn't matter, because there wouldn't be as much fuel. Ron was in heaven because he sat in the "co-pilot" seat with earphones on and eye access to the dials that controlled our fate. The plane was equipped with a Global Positioning System that took its readings from a satellite. We could follow exactly where we were because our blip was on a moving map. When we flew over volcanos we knew which ones

The Grumman Goose turbo-prop with pilot Mark Greig, Estelle and Ron

they were and how high they jutted upward.

The Aleutian chain is full of volcanos, some looking like craters inside of craters. None were smoking but many were steaming. We were scrambling to take pictures because we would never again be in such a place. At one point Ron commented that it was cold in

Mark and Ron in the cockpit

the plane so Mark turned on the cabin heat. Sitting in the back with the barrels I noticed that the atmosphere inside the cabin was getting foggy and had a definite odor of fuel. Mark didn't seem concerned. He later explained to Ron that the fumes were from the fuel vaporizing — ominously interesting, I thought.

When we passed over Adak we began to descend, and when we broke through the clouds we were over Kanaga. It looked like a giant golf course — green and hilly with lakes and sand traps. Mark circled the bay and pointed to the monument. I didn't see it, but I did see the remaining buildings and the pilings where the docks and pier once stood.

He flew low over the bay looking for the best shore to pull up to. Because he had never landed in Kanaga Bay, he was unfamiliar with the currents and the terrain. When we landed he put the wing pontoons

Flying into Kanaga Bay; Memorial Point juts into the center from the right.

down and scooted on the water until it looked like he could lower the wheels and run up onto the shore. He tried this at several different places without success and finally turned off the engines. We were about 100 feet from shore.

The water was about waist high and we didn't relish getting into it. So we broke out our "rubber duckie" life raft and blew it up. We tied a nylon cord to it so I could pull it back to the plane after Ron had gotten to shore and then go ashore myself. The cord was about 15 feet short, so Ron got out his "climbing rope" and extended it. There was no smooth beach to land on, and Ron was lodged tight into our "two-child" raft with two heavy day packs. Mark and I were laughing because disembarking was like trying to get out of a hammock. He got wet. We pulled the raft back and I rowed to shore.

Rowing the raft to the shore from the Grumman Goose. Pilot Mark Greig would taxi out into Kanaga Bay.

Mark had said that he'd have to take the plane out into the bay and wait at anchor, because he didn't know how the tides would run. We didn't know where we would be when it was time to go back to the plane, so we decided to carry the raft with us on land.

Ron carried the raft so we wouldn't have to go back and retrieve it if we had to come down in a different spot to meet the plane.

The bank came down to the shoreline. We looked for an opening so we could climb to the top. The tundra was awful to get through. It was about two feet deep and thick, with the summer growth of reeds, flowers and grasses on top of that. We had to lift our feet about two feet at each step — up, out, over and down. We tried walking up the bank but it was hard to get a foothold, so we pulled ourselves up hand over hand. I was carrying the oars and a pack and Ron had the raft on his back over his pack. We had to stop and breathe often. When we were finally on top, we set off for the buildings and the monument. Every step sank down into the tundra and then into the boggy mire under it.

When we got to where the buildings had been, there were two that were still standing, a small cabin and the barn. The barn was in surprisingly good shape. It was eerie to go into it and see the things that Royse had described in his diary. The goat stalls were intact. The feeding bins were right where they should be.

I disdain people who carve their names to establish their immortality, but I was hoping we'd see his name graffitied in the wood. Though there were no names, it was clear there had been other visitors to the island since 1938 — we found some aluminum Pepsi cans and a few other evidences of recent visits.

We looked uphill and saw the monument. It was the strangest feeling to actually see it, although I had seen the picture of it and I knew what was engraved on it. We struggled to the top of the hill, and when we got there I reached out to touch it as if it were a living thing.

We took pictures and we made a crayon rubbing of it. Ron suggested we put the rubbing in a frame when we get home, but I

At the monument to the two men

114

didn't want to display it. I just wanted something to prove I had come to this place.

Behind the monument was a large clump of blue lupine. Somehow that was fitting.

*Lupine on
Kanaga Island*

* * *

We wanted to explore and see if we could find some of the places my father had written about. We did see a "Haystack," a projection in the bay that had tundra growing from the top. We headed for Indian Point to overlook the reef where seals gathered, but we ran out of enthusiasm because it was hard going.

A light rain had begun, but it wasn't cold. When we started back to the buildings, we thought it might be easier to slog through a dell that ran nearby a lake. As soon as we got down there we knew it was a mistake. The tundra wasn't as thick, but the silty mud was like quicksand. It wasn't smart to stop on it.

In his diary Royse talked about measuring the depth of a lake. He said the water was only a few feet deep but the mud went on forever:

"One afternoon Mr. Kellerman and I went out on the ice to sound the depth of the lake. We found about four feet of water and no bottom to the mud. All the valleys here are filled with mud, with a crust of grass on top of them. If the grass is cut through I suppose a person would sink to China, or Hoboken, in the mud."

This lake wasn't deep, but it was easy to envision the two men choosing to walk in the lowland across the winter ice. When it broke beneath them they were carrying guns and shovels. They had heavy boots (two sizes too large) and layers of clothes. There would have been no way for them to free themselves from the mud. They would have died of hypothermia before they drowned.

* * *

Back at the buildings, the small house had only a latch on the door — no lock, so we went in. The term "rude" furnishings occurred to us. There were two bunks and a table. There was also a sink and a faucet. Running water was just history. Outside, the bird pen had fallen down, but it looked like the same coop was there that had housed the three wounded geese. Ron took a photo of me standing where Royse stood in the picture that came home with his effects.

We discovered that we could walk along the shore more easily than we could slog overland. We started yelling to Mark and he moved the

A dilapidated construction of lumber and chicken wire was apparently what remained of the pen where Royse kept his injured geese.

plane toward shore. The tide had come in, so he could get close enough that Ron, already wet, could pull me and the packs in the raft out to the plane.

We took off and flew over the myriad lakes and hills on this wind-blown, forbidding island that for so many years had been but a vague place in our imagination. We hadn't really gone to Kanaga seeking an answer to Royse's disappearance. It was more a pilgrimage to be where he had been, to make real the adventures he described in his letters. And now, for me, although the mystery of his disappearance hadn't been solved, I felt I could finally say good-bye.

The Kindness of Strangers

When we landed at Unalaska and the accountant tallied up the bill, we noticed there was no charge for down time. The woman told us, "We're all so happy that you could do this. We don't want to charge you for it."

As we were leaving to go back to The Bunkhouse, another pilot said to us, "Did you find the monument OK?"

"How did you know?" I said.

"Oh, we all knew. We were hoping the weather would hold for you!"

Later we met a woman who was "the Magistrate" in the community of Unalaska. (I had thought *Magistrate* was a title from English TV shows!) She wanted us to make a videotape of our story to be aired on the Unalaska TV channel. I declined. This had been a very personal odyssey, and although I was touched by the kindness we met everywhere, I felt that to do such a thing would have diminished our pilgrimage.

* * *

After we got home from Kanaga it occurred to us that some of the men who served with my father might still be alive. So Ron contacted the Naval Pensions Department in Washington, D.C. and found that the lieutenant, Ross Kellerman, now 90 years old, was living in a retirement home in Seattle. We wrote and explained our interest in the expedition where my father had last served. He welcomed a visit from us, so we flew to Washington.

When we went to see him, he seemed kind of hostile at first. As things warmed up he explained that it had been his responsibility to make contact with the families of the missing men. "But I'm no good at that sort of thing," he said.

As he relaxed, we asked him about details that wouldn't have been in the official report — the day to day activities and the personalities of the men in the party. We had wondered about Southerland, who was neither radioman nor aerographer. "He was a funny duck. He didn't want to be there. But he was assigned because he could speak Japanese." Then Kellerman explained more about the mission.

Royse's references to the Panay Incident made it clear that the U. S. wasn't oblivious to the Japanese plan for expansion. And if war was inevitable, our response could be through the Aleutian Islands. This would require airfields along the way, and Kanaga's terrain might lend itself to such a base. So the aerographers were assigned to map weather patterns that would determine such construction. The radiomen were assigned to monitor locations of the Japanese fishing boats that frequented the area. Seaman Southerland had grown up in Japan because his parents had been missionaries there.

Southerland had a separate room and wanted nothing to do with the other men. He wasn't clean, and his presence got so offensive that Gibson (the medic) asked permission to give him a "G.I. bath." This meant that the men stripped and scrubbed him down and washed his sheets and clothes.

"It didn't make him any more congenial but at least he didn't smell bad," Kellerman told us.

On the morning that Gibson and Musick left to go seal hunting, they presented themselves to Kellerman so he could check out their equipment. "They were ready with guns and clothing. They explained their planned route — ultimately to the reef where seals sometimes appeared. I didn't worry about them. They had planned it carefully.

"But when they didn't come back I set a lantern on a rise in case they had lost their direction. We had no men to spare for an extended search, but in twos they went so far as to a known cave where, if one of them had been hurt, they might have holed up." But there was no trace.

"I don't know what happened to them. These islands are volcanic and the tundra grass grew over deep caves. They could have fallen and weren't able to get out. If they got to the reef, it's possible that a wave washed them off and they drowned. The lakes were frozen over but they might have fallen through the ice. If they were on the cliff side the wind could have blown them off."

Kellerman radioed for a search party from Bremerton, but the distance and timing wouldn't have allowed for the men to be alive.

Later, in February, the *Swallow*, a supply ship with a crew of 40 men, was dispatched to Kanaga with replacements for Gibson and Musick. It ran aground on a reef, and until a rescue ship came, all 40 men had to be housed in the base's limited accommodations.

When the population overload had been returned to Seattle, Radioman Cunningham "started talking to the ravens" and had to be put under guard. "When I reported the situation to the Seattle base they sent a replacement crew. The following August the Kanaga project was abandoned."

Later, when the Japanese occupied Kiska and Attu and the west end of the island chain, the Americans burned the Kanaga base, which accounted for the charred pilings that marked where the base had been.

I ask Mr. Kellerman about the monument — where did it come from and who designed it?

When the rest of Royse's crew was sent back to Seattle for reassignment, Kellerman went to those in command and asked for some sort of recognition of what had happened. The monument gave no details — just names and dates.

Minesweeper Runs Aground

BREMERTON, Feb. 20 (A.P.)— Naval headquarters announced today the minesweeper Swallow ran hard aground on Kanaga island in the western Aleutians yesterday but that its crew of 40 reached shore safely and that the coast guard cutter Spencer had been ordered to rescue.

Details were scant and they varied in one respect with radio reports received in San Francisco saying a coast guard cutter already had picked up the Swallow's crew.

Kanaga island is 1400 miles west of Seward, Alaska, in the fog-wrapped Aleutian group. The naval aerological station there is one of the most remote outposts flying the American flag.

The Swallow left here Feb. 10 on a "routine" voyage with supplies for the Kanaga weather station.
(Continued on Page 2, Col. 2)

Minesweeper Runs Aground

(Continued from Page One)

composed of 10 men in command of Lt. R. R. Kellerman.

The navy statement said there was no significance in the fact that the Swallow's voyage was seasonally the earliest ever ordered to the remote Bering sea waters.

Aboard the Swallow were Pharmacist's Mate N. P. Stevenson and Ship's Cook Guy V. Stricklin, replacements for Chief Pharmacist's Mate Royse R. Gibson and Ship's Cook Clyde Musick, of the original aerological station detail, who vanished mysteriously on a hunting trip in early January.

The disappearance of Gibson and Musick has not been explained. No distress signals have been sighted.

CREW ESCAPES AS NAVY SHIP RUNS AGROUND

Forty members of the crew of the navy minesweeper Swallow escaped when the vessel ran aground and were rescued yesterday by a coast guard ship from Kanaga island, in the Middle Aleutians.

A newspaper article from February 20, 1938 about the minesweeper Swallow running aground on Kanaga Island while delivering replacements for Royse Gibson and Clyde Musick

When it was shipped back to the island, the new crew, using a sledge, hauled it up the hill to where it now stands.

As our conversation wound down, we asked Kellerman where he was sent after his Kanaga assignment. He served in the Pacific and worked at aerography, his specialty. A sad memory from that time: He was awaiting a planeload of aerographers and watched as the transport crashed within sight of land. Everyone on board was killed.

When we were leaving, Kellerman got pensive. "Gibson was a good man. I was glad to have him for a friend."

And we were glad to have been able to have some further insight into the mystery of Royse's time on Kanaga Island and his disappearance there.

A New Chapter

In 2011 The U. S. Department of Fish & Wildlife embarked on a project to restore the natural habitat of all of the Alaskan islands. So that birds would return and resume their nesting habits, these employees were assigned to trap foxes and relocate them to the mainland. (As late as the 1930s there was a big demand for fox furs, so fox breeders took advantage of the market and populated the islands with these animals.)

William (Billy) Pepper, captain of the research vessel *Tiglax* of the U. S. Fish & Wildlife Alaska Maritime National Wildlife Refuge,* came from headquarters in Homer, Alaska to Kanaga for such a fox-removal project. When he came across the monument, he noticed that the plaque was damaged and had nearly fallen off the granite base. Pepper also noted that there was no information as to how these men died.

---

*The Alaska Maritime National Wildlife Refuge, comprising the Aleutian chain of islands including Kanaga, was established in 1913 as a national reservation for native birds, fur farming, reindeer herding, and development of the fisheries. Jeff Williams, Assistant Manager of the Refuge, explained that in 1937 biological studies showed that fox farming had a deleterious effect on the native ecosystem. Since then the Refuge has restored over 1.5 million acres on almost 50 islands to its fox-free status, before humans introduced them. The environment continues to recover, and the Refuge continues to be managed.

He removed the damaged plaque and got in touch with Dennis Montagna at the National Park Service in Philadelphia, who is responsible for restoring monuments for the Department of the Interior. Someone in Homer remembered the letters Ron had written to the base commander on Adak explaining why we wanted to go to Kanaga.

Dennis phoned us in Lemon Grove, California. His first focus was to restore and re-anchor the plaque to the granite monument. As we talked, he was caught up in the story, intrigued by all the offbeat details. I told him we had made a pilgrimage to Kanaga and also that we had met with Ross Kellerman and been given a personal account of the sequence of events.

When I told him we had made a "memorial book" that included all of my father's letters, he asked if he could borrow it, because this was an unusual story. Two years later he had created a PowerPoint program that he presented at several historical events on the east coast — he mentioned one in Atlantic City.

Dennis decided, after receiving the plaque and talking to restorers, that the original, because of its condition, would be better preserved indoors in a museum setting. A new plaque, better able to withstand the Kanaga weather, was forged in a foundry in Montana. The process started with making a rubber mold from the original plaque.

Over the years the granite at the top corners of the monument base had come apart. So instead of being made with the attaching spikes

PHOTO: PETER OLSON

The original plaque (left) and the new one

in the four corners as the original plaque had been designed, the new plaque's four points of attachment were near the middle of each edge.

When the new plaque was ready, it was burnished and given a chemical patina and a wax coating. In 2013 Billy Pepper and crew installed it on Kanaga.

On June 14, 2013 the plaque was attached to the original granite base on the hill overlooking the site where the aerological station had been. Shown here, left to right, are Andy Velsko, Holly Gaboriault, Michael Mumm and Billy Pepper at the installation.

Also in 2013 we finally met Dennis in person when he and his family came to San Diego. At our home he showed us his PowerPoint program and invited us to be his guests in Chicago that summer, where he was scheduled to present the program.

Since we had already seen it, we decided we wouldn't go to Chicago. But our daughter Jenny and her husband and son made a special pilgrimage and were introduced to the audience.

Dennis had extended his presentation to explain how in 1938 people in the lower 48 states knew little about Alaskan geography. (My uncle Max had said, for instance, "Well, we'll just get a hunting party together and go find him ourselves." And my grandmother found solace in knowing that "Eskimos will take you in if you're lost.")

* * *

By the time you read this, the original plaque and a rendition of the story of the aerological station and the disappearance of Royse Gibson and Clyde Musick will likely be ensconced in the Alaska Islands & Oceans Visitor Center in Homer. Perhaps a copy of this *Kanaga Diary* will join them there.

About the Author

Estelle Gibson grew up in the San Diego County, California mountain town of Julian, and in the desert town of Brawley, in Imperial County. She got to know her future husband, Ron Lauer, at summer dances in Julian when she was a teenager. From 1950 to 1954 Estelle attended College of the Pacific, while her future husband finished his enlistment in the Marine Corps. Estelle became an elementary school teacher. After they married, they traveled extensively in Europe, and then returned to the San Diego area. Ron began his first teaching job, and they started a family and raised their three children. Following a hiatus in her teaching career, Estelle returned to it in 1980, this time as a teacher of English as a Second Language. Upon their retirement in 1995, Estelle and Ron began traveling again, and Estelle also turned to writing.

Kanaga Diary is **Estelle Gibson Lauer's** fifth book, her first with Dayton Publishing. *A Century of Gibsons* (1999, a history of her father's family), *Maturation Rites* (2015, a memoir of her college days), and *The Story of Adam and Eve* and *The Story of Noah and His Ark* (2017, retellings of the Bible stories in modern settings) were self-published.